THE QUESTIONS
AN OUTDOOR SCIENTIST ASKS

Have you ever wondered what makes moss the color of emeralds? (Hint: it has to do with chlorophyll.) Or for that matter, what makes emeralds the color of emeralds? (Hint: it has to do with the presence of chemical elements chromium and vanadium.) Have you ever collected and identified different types of leaves or figured out why some trees flower in May and others in August? Have you ever dissected an acorn? One summer not too long ago, I puzzled over how smashed-up clamshells wound up on the road to the beach. Then one day, I observed a seagull drop a clam on the road, then wait for a car to run it over like a giant nutcracker, busting open the clamshell for the bird to eat the soft meat inside. Mystery explained! I'm still trying to figure out how the red fox I saw in my doctor's parking lot got there. Was it lost? Frightened? Were there babies nearby? Would it attack if approached? You may not always find the answer, but these are the questions an outdoor scientist asks about the world.

ALSO BY TEMPLE GRANDIN

THE OUTDOOR SCIENTIST

The Wonder of Observing the Natural World

TEMPLE GRANDIN

WITH BETSY LERNER

PHILOMEL BOOKS

PHILOMEL BOOKS
An imprint of Penguin Random House LLC, New York

First published in the United States of America by Philomel, an imprint of Penguin Random House LLC, 2021
First paperback edition published 2022

Visit us online at penguinrandomhouse.com.

THE LIBRARY OF CONGRESS HAS CATALOGED THE HARDCOVER EDITION AS FOLLOWS:
Names: Grandin, Temple, author. I Lerner, Betsy, author.
Title: The outdoor scientist : the wonder of observing the natural world /
Temple Grandin with Betsy Lerner.
Description: New York : Philomel Books, 2021. I Includes bibliographical
references and index. I Audience: Ages 8–12 I Audience: Grades 3–7 I
Summary: "A guide to exploring the outdoors and asking questions about
nature"—Provided by publisher.
Identifiers: LCCN 2020047611 I ISBN 9780593115558 (hardcover) I ISBN
9780593115572 (ebook)
Subjects: LCSH: Nature—Juvenile literature. I Natural history—Juvenile
literature. I Nature—Miscellanea—Juvenile literature.
Classification: LCC QH48 .G79 2021 I DDC 508—dc23
LC record available at https://lccn.loc.gov/2020047611

Manufactured in Canada

ISBN 9780593115565

10 9 8 7 6 5 4 3

FRI

Edited by Jill Santopolo and Talia Benamy
Design by Monique Sterling
Text set in Granjon LT Std

To all the children inspired by nature

CONTENTS

INTRODUCTION

As a child, my world was divided into two places: inside and outside. It was the 1950s, and if we had any say, my siblings and I preferred to play outside. We just loved being outdoors, whether it was the neighborhood with its playgrounds or our backyard or the woods beyond. Anything we found outside was fair game for our entertainment: we made daisy chains, pressed flowers, built tree houses out of scrap lumber. We also flew kites and raced our bikes. I could spend an entire day on my bike pretending it was a horse or a car or a rocket. I can still remember summer nights when the sun set late, and my mother would call to us from the screen door to get inside. Her voice would get increasingly irritated, as it was almost impossible to drag us away from our games of kick the can, four square, hopscotch, and double Dutch jump rope (which I was terrible at). Another reason I didn't like going inside: I dreaded bath time. My mother would be shocked at the layers of grime and filth from a day of playing outdoors. To me, they were a badge of honor.

The outdoors is where I first started making discoveries, though I never would have called them that. I never would have thought that splitting rocks, or collecting shells, or dissecting flower buds was something scientists did to unravel Earth's mysteries. To my mind, I was just playing. It's only looking back now that I see how curiosity led to observation, and how observation is at the heart of all science. If you like looking at trees, and bark, and the pattern of veins in leaves; if you are fascinated by clouds or the spots on a ladybug's back; if you like to split open rocks and see what's inside, then you're already an outdoor scientist.

I had no idea what I wanted to be when I grew up, a question that grown-ups are fairly obsessed with. I also had no idea that all the stuff I loved doing as a kid would come to inform my life's work. I'm an animal scientist, a professor, and an engineer, which means that I study animals and teach college students, but I also work with cows, designing livestock equipment. This book traces how my childhood interests contributed to my work today. I also include lots of stories of scientists who, as you will see, saw their childhood interest develop into passion that they pursued for their entire lives. A young Mary Anning would discover the first complete skeleton of an *Ichthyosaurus*, an ancient sea creature, on the cliffs of England and become one of the leading paleontologists of her day. Jacques Cousteau always wanted to fly, but a childhood accident ended that dream. Instead he became one of the great underwater explorers, who would later describe swimming underwater like flying. You've probably heard that the number of rings in a tree tells its age. That's something we know thanks to Andrew Ellicott Douglass, whose early interest in astronomy and observations about climate change led him to develop a new branch of science called dendrochronology. Irene Pepperberg got a parakeet as a gift when she was a young child and would spend her life studying whether birds could just mimic us or truly understand speech. Katherine Johnson was a math genius who would overcome racial injustice and discrimination at

NASA to become one of a small group of Black women who came up with the calculations to get Apollo 11 not only to the moon, but back.

But it was during the summers at my aunt's ranch, where we spent most of the days outdoors, that my love of the natural world and interest in animal science came together. We'd spend whole days outside with the horses going on long trail rides. It was really hot and my aunt used to say that we were opening a door to an oven in the morning when we set out. The grass was brown, and she'd say "everything will green up" when the big downpours came. I loved watching the thunderheads build up in anticipation of the rain. It was like a huge drama in the sky that I could stare at for hours. I later learned in earth science class that thunderheads (also known as cumulonimbus clouds) form when a body of hot air meets a body of cold air. When the two meet, the hot air rises, creating thunderheads. They can reach heights of 50,000 feet above the surface of the earth. The heat released by water condensation causes powerful rain, lightning, and winds. I loved learning about stuff like that.

Above all, this book is about looking at things closely, about observation—the scientist's most important tool. It's about being a detective like Sherlock Holmes and noticing what others fail to notice. The best part is you don't need any special or fancy equipment, you don't need to remember a charger, you just need your eyes and the power of observation. Are there one or two sets of paw prints in the snow? Three or four kinds of birds having a conversation in a grove? What kinds of plants are strong enough to push their way through the cracks in the sidewalk? Imagine having concrete poured over your head! How would you escape? For plants, the secret is water. When water enters a plant cell by osmosis, the pressure pushes the plant upward, giving it the power to break through asphalt or concrete.

Have you ever wondered what makes moss the color of emeralds? (Hint: it has to do with chlorophyll.) Or for that matter, what makes emeralds the color of emeralds? (Hint: it has to do with the presence of chemical elements chromium and vanadium.) Have you ever collected and identified different types of leaves or figured out why some trees flower in May and others in August? Have you ever dissected an acorn? One summer not too long ago, I puzzled over how smashed-up clamshells wound up on the road to the beach. Then one day, I observed a seagull drop a clam on the road, then wait for a car to run it over like a giant nutcracker, busting open the clamshell for the bird to eat the soft meat inside. Mystery explained! I'm still trying to figure out how the red fox I saw in my doctor's parking lot got there. Was it lost? Frightened? Were there babies nearby? Would it attack if approached? You may not always find the answer, but these are the questions an outdoor scientist asks about the world.

Today, more than ever, you can participate in the great global project known as citizen science. All over the world, volunteers donate their time, energy, and passion to collect data about the world around them. This is also called crowdsourcing, connecting millions of people to share information about a given topic. These efforts contribute to our knowledge of the earth and all living things. Citizen scientists help scientists collect data on contamination in the environment, measure levels of climate change and pollution, and track endangered species as well as those populations rapidly growing. You can go to citizenscience.gov/catalog to survey all the different ways you can get involved as an outdoor scientist.

Photo courtesy of the author

From a young age, I loved hunting for treasure on the beach. A feather was definitely treasure.

I hope, as you read this book, you find projects and experiments that intrigue you and lead you on your own scientific journey into the natural world.

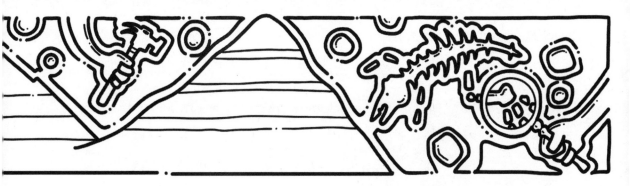

ROCKS

CHAPTER ONE

When we were young, my sister and I loved to bust rocks open in our backyard in Dedham, Massachusetts. We would find them under bushes, in the fields beyond our house, or alongside brooks. Some rocks looked the same on the inside as the outside, but some contained bright-colored crystals within. Once I saw those colors inside, I had to bust open as many rocks as possible. I think I spent an entire summer busting rocks open. I mostly used a hammer since I didn't have a chisel. Sometimes, I'd just smash one rock against another or against the pavement. (If you're going to try this yourself, and I highly encourage you to do so, it's essential to wear safety goggles, which can be purchased at your local hardware store.)

In grade school, I learned that the rocks we loved were called geodes. A geode is basically any rock with a cavity of crystals inside. My aunt wore a crystal necklace that I always admired. For Christmas one year, she gave

I loved cracking open rocks to find the colors inside.

me a crystal as a gift. I loved watching rainbows ping in all directions when the sun hit it. At the American Museum of Natural History in New York City, I was amazed by the crystals I saw, the dazzling colors and formations. Some looked like fireworks, exploding in all directions. Others looked like undersea creatures. I had never seen so many brilliant colors and color combinations.

One way crystals form is when magma, or liquid rock, begins to cool. Different kinds and colors of crystals will form depending on factors like the temperature of the liquid and the amount of time the liquid takes to cool. It's the same process with snowflakes, also known as snow crystals. They are made of molecules that form in repeating patterns. You can observe crystallization up close if you leave a solution of water and salt out all night at room temperature. The water will evaporate, and the salt will crystallize.

WARNING: Adult supervision required for boiling water.

PROJECT # 1
MAKE YOUR OWN CRYSTAL

You'll need:
- Pot to boil water
- 1 ¾ cups water
- ½ cup crystal or Epsom salt
- Glass jar or large glass

- Food coloring (optional)
- Thick string
- Pencil, butter knife, Popsicle stick, or any thin stick

INSTRUCTIONS

① BRING WATER TO A BOIL IN A POT (ADULTS CAN HELP WITH THIS IF YOU'RE NOT ALLOWED TO USE THE STOVE YOURSELF).

② STIR IN SALT, ADDING UNTIL IT NO LONGER DISSOLVES. THE WATER SHOULD LOOK ALMOST CLEAR WITH A FEW GRAINS OF SALT SWIRLING AROUND (WHICH MEANS YOU'VE ADDED SLIGHTLY MORE SALT THAN THE WATER CAN ABSORB).

③ TRANSFER THE SOLUTION TO A JAR.

④ ADD A FEW DROPS OF FOOD COLORING IF YOU WANT TO MAKE COLORED CRYSTALS.

⑤ TIE ONE END OF YOUR STRING AROUND THE MIDDLE OF YOUR PENCIL AND LOWER THE OTHER END OF THE STRING INTO THE JAR. THE STRING SHOULD BE LONG ENOUGH SO THAT IT ALMOST TOUCHES THE BOTTOM OF YOUR JAR.

⑥ BALANCE THE PENCIL ACROSS THE TOP OF YOUR JAR.

⑦ CRYSTALS SHOULD START TO FORM IN ONE OR TWO DAYS.

Improvise: Try using pipe cleaners instead of string and shape them into hearts, moons, lollipops, or other shapes.

You can also do this experiment using sugar instead of salt to make edible rock candy. The ratio for that is 3 cups of sugar for every 1 cup of water.

Once in a great while, as my sister and I were searching for interesting stones, we'd find stones with rings around them, and we called these our "lucky stones" or "wishing stones." These we did not smash. Instead, we proudly displayed them on a shelf in the garage where we collected our treasures, like birds' nests, sea glass, driftwood, and all the things our mother wouldn't allow in the house. I always wanted to know how the rocks got their rings. According to Dr. Jeremy Young at University College London, rocks have veins that can fill with a liquid containing quartz or calcite, both of which have a white color. Rings can also form when a rock cracks. He explained that the liquid can either dissolve (disappear) or precipitate (turn into a solid). If it precipitates, a white ring is formed.

We had an encyclopedia at home that I used to identify all the different kinds of rocks you could find in the Northeast. Now you can get the same information on the internet, or by visiting your local library. But all you need to start identifying the rocks where you live is . . . a rock. If you have a backyard, dig up a few there.

A polished wishing stone from my personal collection.

Photo by Temple Grandin

If you live in an apartment without a yard, try your nearby park or schoolyard.

There are three main groups of rocks:

1. Igneous rocks are formed when magma, which is molten (liquid) rock beneath the surface of the earth, cools and becomes solid. The most common igneous rock is granite, and there is lots of it where we lived in New England. Granite doesn't have much texture or

layering. It usually has a hard, smooth surface and is mostly made of black, white, or gray materials with mica flecks (the shiny stuff that looks like bits of mirror). It is used to make everything from skyscrapers and statues to kitchen countertops. There is a really cool type of granite called orbicular. I wish I could have found some of this in New England.

2. Sedimentary rocks generally have layers, are sandy to the touch, and are usually brown and gray. The layers of sedimentary rock that make up huge parts of the Grand Canyon, for example, are created by sand and rock pushed around by wind and water and compacted over the span of millions of years. If you're really lucky, you might find a fossil with an animal footprint or a leaf in a sedimentary rock. Limestone, sandstone, and halite (which is salt) are among the most common sedimentary rocks and are used in construction materials like cement. Other sedimentary rocks, like coal, are mined to produce energy.

I found this orbicular granite in a science classroom.

Photo by Temple Grandin

3. Metamorphic rock forms when sedimentary, igneous, or even other metamorphic rocks are transformed by extreme pressure and heat. Metamorphic rocks include varieties like schist and slate, but the most famous is marble. These rocks tend to have smooth surfaces or curved layers. Marble has been used in some of the most well-known

buildings in the world, including the Pantheon in Rome, Italy; the Taj Mahal in Agra, India; and a number of U.S. capital buildings and monuments, including the Washington Monument, the Lincoln Memorial, and the Supreme Court building.

ARE MARBLES MADE OF MARBLE?

Good question. Marbles have been around since ancient Egypt and have been found in places as varied as Pompeii and the Native American (specifically Cherokee) plains. According to Rob Lammle of Mental Floss, the first marbles were probably small stones smoothed over by rushing streams or ocean waves. Early marbles were also made from clay, bones, acorns, and walnuts. Later, marbles were made from marble stone, which is known for its beautiful swirls of color and is likely how they got their name.

For some reason I don't completely understand, humans have always enjoyed flicking round objects in an effort to knock their opponents out. Other games that use the same principle, but with larger balls, are bocce and billiards.

In 1902, an Ohio man named Martin Frederick Christensen patented the first machine for mass manufacturing glass marbles, which he called "Machine for Making Spherical Bodies or Balls." His method is still in use today. Glass is melted into liquid that flows out of the kiln and is cut into small pieces called slugs. The slugs are dropped onto spinning cast-iron rolls that shape the ball. Marbles come in lots of colors with beautiful patterns. The effects are created by adding colored glass while the marble is still in a liquid form, then twisting or rolling the ball to swirl the color inside. Marbles have fun names that describe their features, such as bumblebees, corkscrews, swirls, cat's eyes, and clouds. The answer to our original question? No, marbles these days are usually not made of marble.

To measure a rock or mineral's hardness, geologists use something called the Mohs' scale, created by Friedrich Mohs in 1812. Mohs was interested in geology (the scientific field that studies rocks, minerals, and solid earth) from an early age and worked with minerals his whole life. But he is best known for the ten-point scale he developed to classify minerals and rocks by their hardness, which geologists still use today. The softest mineral is talc and the hardest is a diamond. The Mohs' scale basically creates its rankings by way of a scratch test. Here are the guidelines:

- If you can scratch a rock with your **fingernail** and leave a mark, it's 1–2.5 on the Mohs' scale.
- If can scratch the rock with a **copper penny**, it's a 3–3.5 on the scale.
- If you can scratch a rock with a **knife**, it's 4–5.5 on the scale.
- If you can scratch it with a **steel nail**, it's a 6–6.5 on the scale.
- If you can scratch it with a **drill bit**, it's a 7–8.5 on the scale.
- And if even the drill doesn't make a scratch, then your rock is somewhere between an 8.5 and a 10.

Here are the basics to look for in rock identification:

- **Color:** Note the color and the shades. Be specific. For instance, if your rock is gray, note the shades from light to dark.
- **Markings:** Does your rock have stripes, dots, or other markings?
- **Luster:** This is your rock's sheen. Is it shiny or dull? Sometimes a rock can be both: shiny in one part and dull in another.
- **Mineral Habits:** This is the shape of your rock, its layers and textures. Does it have weird crags, depressions, or bumps?
- **Cleavage and Fracture:** This is how the rock breaks. When you smash it, do you get a clean break or does it splinter off? What does the inside look like?

Once you've conducted a full investigation of your rock, you will be ready to make an identification. The final step is to check your observations against a guide to rocks and minerals either from the library or online to make an accurate identification. Two reliable guides I can recommend are *Smithsonian Handbooks: Rocks and Minerals* by Chris Pellant and *Ultimate Explorer Field Guide: Rocks and Minerals* by Nancy Honovich. Don't be discouraged if you don't get it right at first—many rocks have similar features, and it takes some practice to make a positive identification. The fun part is honing your rock detective skills. The more rocks you examine, the better you'll get at it.

PROJECT # 2
ROCK & CRYSTAL SPECIMEN BOX

Start your own rock collection or specimen box. Visit the local library or use the internet to look up a list of rocks in your area and their properties. Think of this as a scavenger hunt for different kinds of rocks.

You'll need:

- Marker
- Shoebox lid
- Guide for identifying rocks (either a book or a website)
- Glue or epoxy

- Magnifying glass or microscope (If you don't have a magnifier or microscope, your parents might have some magnifying eyeglasses at home. They work well, too.)

INSTRUCTIONS

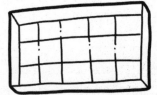

① DRAW A GRID OF 15 BOXES LIKE A TIC-TAC-TOE GRID ON THE INSIDE OF YOUR SHOEBOX LID.

② USE YOUR GUIDE TO LABEL EACH BOX WITH THE NAME OF A DIFFERENT ROCK FROM YOUR AREA AND ITS PROPERTIES.

③ SEARCH YOUR NEIGHBORHOOD FOR ROCK "SAMPLES." THINK OF IT LIKE FILLING IN THE NUMBERS ON A BINGO CARD: THE GOAL IS TO GET A SAMPLE OF EACH ROCK IN YOUR AREA.

④ USE A MAGNIFIER TO IDENTIFY THE TEXTURE, COLOR, AND APPEARANCE: IS IT SOLID, MIXED, OR STRIPED? WHAT IS THE HARDNESS ACCORDING TO THE MOHS' SCALE? CAN YOU SCRATCH IT WITH YOUR FINGERNAIL? A PENNY?

⑤ CHECK YOUR IDENTIFICATION AGAINST YOUR GUIDE TO ROCKS AND MINERALS. WITH A POSITIVE IDENTIFICATION, YOU ARE READY TO GLUE IT IN ITS RIGHTFUL BOX WITH THE NAME AND DESCRIPTION, AND YOU'RE ON YOUR WAY.

ROCKS IN YOUR HEAD

Eugene Shoemaker started collecting rock samples when he was young. He'd been given a bag of marbles, and that started his search for interesting rocks and minerals around his neighborhood. In fifth grade, he took a class at the Buffalo Museum of Science, where he first learned about botany, mineralogy, and geology. He read every book he could find in the library on the subject and filled coffee cans with rock samples from the North Platte River near his grandparents' home in Wyoming during summer vacations.

After college, Gene went to work for the United States Geographical Survey. It was the perfect job for a young man who had spent his childhood summers rock hunting. Gene Shoemaker traveled the country keeping track of various landscapes and locating natural resources. In the 1960s, he was assigned to study the Hopi Buttes in Arizona, where he came across an enormous crater. Until then, most scientists believed that all craters were formed by volcanic activity. Gene Shoemaker was the first person to prove that some of the craters on Earth and the moon were formed from the impact of a space rock or meteorite crashing down from space. This became known as "impact theory," and it was later used to help explain how dinosaurs became extinct. Shoemaker said, "For a long while, nobody believed me, but eventually I convinced them."

Gene Shoemaker's lifelong dream was to go to the moon. An illness disqualified him from becoming the first geologist in space, but he was hired to work on the Apollo 11 expedition, training astronauts on lunar missions. Apollo 11 was the first mission to put men on the moon, and it was Shoemaker's greatest disappointment not to go with them. After Gene died, a student of his made sure that some of his ashes were put on a spacecraft designed to crash into the moon. To this day, Gene Shoemaker is the only person to have his ashes spread on the moon. So, you could say, he fulfilled his dream of going to the moon.

Photo courtesy of the U.S. Geological Survey

Gene Shoemaker surveying land.

The first time I went to Hawaii, I remember flying into an airport on one of the islands and thinking that it looked like a moonscape, except that a fancy hotel and golf course had been built on the hardened lava bed. I had first learned about the earth's layers in fifth-grade geology class. Volcanoes fascinated me in part because of their awesome power, but also because looking down into them was like being able to peer into the earth's crust. Years later, in another part of Hawaii, I traveled with one of my students to look at an active volcano. In the distance, we could see it erupting, and we could only get so close in our car because the road and surrounding area were covered by hardened lava. I got out, walked along the pavement, and then stepped up about a foot onto the solidified lava field. It looked like a pool of black pancake batter had been poured onto both the landscape and the road. Magma that reaches the earth's surface is called lava and glows red and white from the heat. When it cools, it turns black or gray. I was standing on a surface covered in cooled lava.

There are three kinds of volcanoes: active (currently or recently erupting), dormant (hasn't erupted in a long time, but still might), and extinct (hasn't erupted in thousands of years, and likely won't erupt again). It's an incredible natural occurrence when a volcano erupts. Because magma is lighter than solid rock, it rises toward the earth's surface. As it rises, gas that had been dissolved in the magma forms bubbles, which help push the magma upward. If the force of the bubbles is strong enough, the magma pushes through the earth's surface—that's what we're seeing when a volcano erupts.

Magma can be created in two ways. When the tectonic plates (the pieces of rock that form the earth's crust) collide, one plate will push the other downward into the mantle (the layer below the crust), which creates new magma that can rise to the surface and spout out of a volcano. Or when the plates pull apart, magma may also rise up to the earth's surface.

FOR THE LOVE OF ROCKS

In 1942, when George Patrick Leonard Walker was sixteen years old, he wrote in his notebook, "Today my interest in Geology began, when I bought my first book on the subject— 'GEOLOGY FOR BEGINNERS' by W.W. Watts. The cost to me was only four and sixpence. I had merely bought this book to learn some of the rudiments of this science, but never intended to study Geology as a science in great detail." Though there were no active volcanoes in Northern Ireland, where Walker grew up, he went on to study every volcano in the world and was a leading geologist and volcanologist (yes, this is a real word) who changed the way scientists study volcanoes. Using Watts's book, he identified volcanic residue in a chalk quarry near his home, then spent as much time as he could exploring the outdoors, searching for geological wonders. By the time he left for college, he was already taking extensive field notes and mapping the places where he found dried-up magma in the surrounding rock.

George is most famous for his hypotheses on volcano formation

Courtesy of Colin J.N. Wilson

and lava flow. He studied places where the flow had cooled down and become part of the landscape. He created a system still used today that shows how strong a volcanic eruption was by studying the hardened lava and identifying properties like graininess, hardness, color, etc. This finding, like Shoemaker's impact theory, also helped scientists figure out when and how dinosaurs became extinct.

George Walker on a 1979 dig in New Zealand.

It wasn't until college that I learned about paleontology, which is the study of ancient nonhuman life on Earth. And by ancient, I mean between 11,000 and four billion years old. Paleontologists are a type of geologist who study fossils (preserved remains of plants and animal bones) to learn more about climates and environments of the past. Animal fossils, including dinosaur bones, are the remains of creatures who died at least 11,000 years ago, and often much longer ago than that. Fossils are made when mud, lava, or sand covers the animal's bones and preserves them. Animals with skeletons or shells are usually the ones that leave behind fossils. Their bones decompose slowly, which leaves time for minerals in the surrounding sediment to seep into the bones and fossilize them.

When paleontologists look at fossils, they can tell what the world was like thousands, millions, sometimes billions of years ago. The skeleton of a megalodon, an extinct shark that was larger than the great white sharks of today, was found in the state of Utah, which is hundreds of miles from the ocean. How did it get there? Some scientists hypothesize that Utah was once under water. Paleontologists are not only looking at fossils for what they tell us about life on Earth, but for what they tell us about the earth itself.

FOSSIL FACE

It was in the mid-1940s in Queens, New York, when Stephen J. Gould's mother realized early on that her son might be a scientist. When other young boys were chasing waves, she recalled how Stephen would go the beach not only to collect shells but to classify them as well, separating them into categories: regular, extraordinary, and unusual. But it was at age five, when Stephen's father first took him to the American Museum of Natural History in New York City, that he encountered the skeleton of a *Tyrannosaurus rex*, which would set the course of his entire life. "I had no idea there were such things," he said. "I was awestruck." He decided on the spot to devote his life to studying dinosaurs and other ancient fossil records. Stephen's obsession with dinosaurs earned him the nickname "fossil face" among his grade-school peers. That didn't stop him from pursuing his passion.

He is best known for developing, with fellow paleontologist Niles Eldredge, the theory of punctuated equilibrium, sometimes shortened to "punk eke." Punk eke challenges Charles Darwin's theory of evolution, also known as "survival of the fittest," which argues that change happens slowly over millions of years and favors species best equipped to adapt to different conditions. Gould and Eldredge believed that for some species, adaptations or changes happen in short bursts with long periods of stability in between. Their theory is still being debated by scientists. What's interesting to me is how ideas themselves evolve. It's up to every new generation of scientists to challenge theories of the past in service of finding truth and new discoveries. The core of scientific truth: observe, hypothesize, test.

SHE SELLS SEASHELLS BY THE SEASHORE

Imagine you live in Dorset, England, near the cliffs of Lyme Regis in the early 1800s. You're around twelve years old and walking around the massive cliffs made of shale and limestone (which you know are sedimentary rocks), and you come upon some bones. Some pretty big bones. That's what happened to Mary Anning and her brother when they were collecting seashells to help supplement the family income. Her brother found the skull, but it was Mary, determined to find the remaining bones, who eventually uncovered the first complete skeleton of an *Ichthyosaurus*, an ancient sea creature.

Mary Anning collecting sea shells with her pike and wicker basket.

A page from Mary Anning's diary of her landmark discovery of the fossil Plesiosaur.

Mary would go on to find the first *Plesiosaurus* skeleton, and the skeletons of a number of other prehistoric animals. Two kids exploring the cliffs near their home provided scientists with a fuller understanding of Earth's history. Most of the history books have forgotten Mary Anning. The nineteenth century often forgot the contributions of women. But Mary's discoveries led to the beginnings of paleontology and changed the way people thought about extinction. Stephen Gould said that she was "probably the most important unsung (or inadequately sung) collecting force in the history of paleontology." One more thing: there are still tons of fossils and bones to be found in Lyme Regis. Families and students go all the time with their chisels and hammers in search of treasure in the cliffs.

Here's a fun fact: it is said that Mary Anning is the inspiration for the tongue twister "She sells seashells by the seashore."

FAKE FOSSIL

You'll need:

- 2 cups flour (plus a few extra tablespoons)
- 1 cup salt
- Large mixing bowl
- 1 cup water
- Mixing spoon
- Wooden board

- Food coloring (red, yellow, and blue)
- Rolling pin
- Drinking glass
- Small plastic toy dinosaurs, shells, leaves, fish or chicken bones, or anything similarly sized

INSTRUCTIONS

❶ MIX THE FLOUR AND SALT TOGETHER IN YOUR MIXING BOWL.

❷ SLOWLY ADD THE WATER, STIRRING WITH YOUR SPOON AS YOU GO.

❸ WHEN THE CONSISTENCY IS LIKE COOKIE DOUGH, REMOVE AND KNEAD ON YOUR BOARD.

TIP: KNEADING WILL BE EASIER IF YOU DUST THE BOARD AND YOUR HANDS WITH EXTRA FLOUR.

❹ ADD ONE DROP OF RED FOOD COLORING, TEN DROPS OF YELLOW, AND ONE DROP OF DARK BLUE TO MAKE THE DOUGH LOOK LIKE DIRT. AS ALWAYS, FEEL FREE TO EXPERIMENT WITH YOUR OWN FORMULA.

❺ ROLL THE DOUGH OUT WITH THE ROLLING PIN UNTIL IT'S 1/2 TO 1 INCH THICK.

❻ USE THE DRINKING END OF YOUR GLASS TO CUT CIRCLES IN THE DOUGH.

❼ BE CREATIVE: PRESS LITTLE PLASTIC DINOSAURS INTO THE DOUGH CIRCLES. TRY SHELLS, LEAVES, BONES FROM A FISH OR CHICKEN, OR ANYTHING YOU'D LIKE. THESE ARE YOUR FOSSIL IMPRESSIONS. ONCE THE ITEM HAS MADE AN IMPRESSION IN THE DOUGH, REMOVE IT.

❽ LET YOUR FOSSIL AIR DRY FOR A COUPLE OF DAYS UNTIL IT'S ROCK HARD.

My siblings and I never discovered anything as remotely fascinating as an *Ichthyosaurus*. In 2019, in Colorado, a team of paleontologists discovered thousands of fossils that belonged to small mammals like pigs and wolves. Dr. Tyler Lyson, who had been hunting fossils since he was ten, had a eureka moment. He had been looking for bones sticking out of the ground when he remembered that rocks called "concretions" held fossils. "I found this ugly white-looking rock that looked like it had a little mammal jaw coming out of it." Lyson cracked it open and found a partial crocodile fossil. He returned with a team, and so far, they've found over 1,000 vertebrate fossils and sixteen different mammal species. What's especially interesting about this find is that it supplies information about how mammals and plant life evolved after the dinosaurs became extinct. A high school student on the dig found the first fossil legume—it was a bean!

We loved to search for rocks and play with them in any way that occurred to us. One of my all-time favorite activities was skipping stones into lakes. You need to find the flattest, thinnest stone. Hold it horizontally between your thumb and index finger. Then flick it really hard onto the surface of the water. When you get it just right, the stone will skim the water, jump up, and jump again. Two elements are key to skipping stones: spin and flatness. Spinning the stone as you pitch it stabilizes it as it flies through the air. The flatness of the stone causes it to bounce when it hits the relatively still surface of the water. The bounce both slows down the stone and propels it back up to skip again. The world record for the greatest number of skips is fifty-one. I think mine was four.

We also used rocks for everything from borders around our campfires to building forts and making mosaic designs. People have been using rocks, glass, and tile to create art for over 4,000 years. Early mosaics were made of small black-and-white squares a little smaller than Scrabble tiles. The tiles were fitted closely together in a bed of mortar, which consisted of soft mud or clay and sand, and was used the same way we use cement to hold bricks and tiles together. A mixture of liquid mortar was used to fill in any gaps. Eventually, mosaics became more elaborate, depicting mythological subjects, religious scenes, and magnificent geometrical designs decorating the domes, roofs, and archways of the world's greatest cathedrals.

PROJECT # 4
PEBBLE MOSAIC

You'll need:

- Fabric tape or regular tape (Fabric tape is easier to reposition or lift off.)
- Tracing paper
- Design from a magazine or the internet (or your own imagination)
- Cardboard or shoebox lid

- Graphite pencil
- Eraser
- Glue
- Pebbles (You can also use dried beans or uncooked rice.)
- Tweezers (optional)
- Q-tips (optional)

INSTRUCTIONS

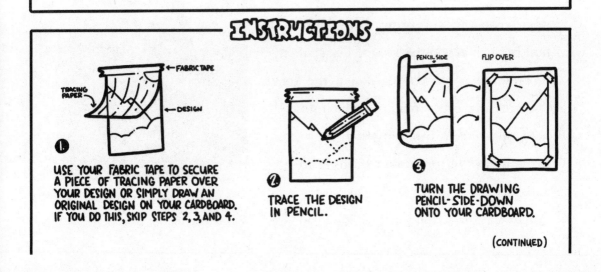

1. USE YOUR FABRIC TAPE TO SECURE A PIECE OF TRACING PAPER OVER YOUR DESIGN OR SIMPLY DRAW AN ORIGINAL DESIGN ON YOUR CARDBOARD. IF YOU DO THIS, SKIP STEPS 2, 3, AND 4.

2. TRACE THE DESIGN IN PENCIL.

3. TURN THE DRAWING PENCIL-SIDE-DOWN ONTO YOUR CARDBOARD.

(CONTINUED)

④ USING AN ERASER, RUB THE LINES SO THEY TRANSFER TO YOUR CARDBOARD. (YOU MAY WANT TO USE FABRIC TAPE HERE, TOO, SO THE PAPER DOESN'T SLIP.)

⑤. NOW THAT YOUR DESIGN IS TRANSFERRED, SPREAD GLUE TO COVER ONE SECTION AT A TIME, AND THEN FILL IT IN WITH PEBBLES.

TIP: BEFORE GLUING, ARRANGE THE PEBBLES TO MAKE SURE THEY FIT AND YOU LIKE THE LAYOUT. IF YOUR PEBBLES ARE TINY, YOU MAY WANT TO USE TWEEZERS.

⑥. FILL IN ANY GAPS WITH MORE GLUE WHEN YOU ARE DONE. IF THE GAPS ARE NARROW, YOU MAY WANT TO USE A Q-TIP. THE GLUE WILL DRY AND MAKE THE PART OF YOUR CARDBOARD BETWEEN YOUR PEBBLES LOOK SHINY.

Another project we loved was building tall stacks of rocks called cairns. Cairns have been around a long time and have had many uses: monuments, landmarks, trail markers, and decorations. Lots of people build cairns in the woods or on the beach and leave them for others to come upon. You can also bring rocks home and build a cairn in your backyard. The challenge of building a cairn is balancing the rocks without any other materials, like glue, to help, piling them from largest at the bottom to smallest at the top. You can also get creative and balance the rocks in the shape of a pyramid or column so long as they don't collapse.

Wikimedia Commons/Tinelot Wittermans

If I had come upon this cairn as a child, I would have been amazed at how it held together without cement or mortar.

CAIRNS

You'll need:

- Rocks in all different sizes

You won't need:

- Glue (or anything else at all)

INSTRUCTIONS

START WITH YOUR LARGEST ROCKS AT THE BOTTOM AND BUILD YOUR WAY UP, USING SMALLER ROCKS THE HIGHER YOU GO.

NOTE: THIS REQUIRES BALANCE AND FITTING THE SURFACE OF THE ROCKS TOGETHER SO THEY DON'T TUMBLE.

START ⟶ ⟶ FINISH

IDEALLY, BUILD YOUR CAIRN AT THE BEACH OR IN THE WOODS FOR OTHERS TO FIND. OTHERWISE, BRING A FEW ROCKS HOME EVERY TIME YOU FIND SOME AND SAVE THEM UP UNTIL YOU HAVE ENOUGH TO BUILD A CAIRN.

Rocks have histories. If they could talk, they would tell us their age, how they wound up in a field or skyscraper, and what they're made of. I've always been curious about pretty much everything in nature, especially when some sleuthing was required. Growing up in New England, we'd come upon lots of abandoned stone walls in the woods while hiking. I always wondered how they got there and why someone would build a stone wall in the woods. It turns out that during the last ice age, glaciers (masses of ice that formed from the accumulation of snow) moved across the East Coast and left tons of rocks. In order to till the soil and grow crops, the farmers had to clear their fields of rocks, which they then used to make the stone wall boundaries. But then something strange happened. Rocks they had cleared in the fall seemed to reappear in the spring. According to author Susan Allport, "People in the Northeast thought that the devil had put them there." They were also nicknamed "New England potatoes" by the farmers for the way they just appeared out of the earth. Science would later explain the process known as "frost heave," which is when the soil freezes and thaws, causing the rocks to shift and get pushed up out of the ground.

The next time you're in a building or at a kitchen counter made of stone, see if you can identify what kind it is. Is it from a local quarry or imported from another state or country? Colorado State University, where I teach, is very proud of its sandstone buildings, which come from a quarry in Lyons, Colorado. If there is a nearby quarry you can visit, you can observe how stone is cut or blasted out of the earth. Wherever you live, look closely at the sidewalk. In many places, it is flecked with a variety of rocks, like mica, limestone, shale, clay, and slate. Stones are used to bind the cement. Once you start thinking about rocks, you'll notice them everywhere.

Rocks were briefly celebrities in 1975 when Gary Dahl, an advertising copywriter, got an idea while listening to his friends complain about their pets and all the work involved in taking care of them. He "invented" a pet that required no care at all: a pet rock. He packaged a rock in a pet carrier with straw and breathing holes. He included a manual called "The Care and Training of Your Pet Rock." It was really just a marketing scheme, but a successful one. He priced them at $4 and sold over 1.5 million pet rocks.

PROJECT # 6
ROCK PET

You'll need:

- Scissors or precision blade
- Carrier (This can be a shoebox or any box with a top.)

- Shredded crepe paper
- Permanent marker
- Rock

INSTRUCTIONS

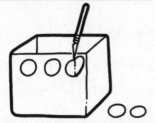

1 USING SCISSORS OR A PRECISION BLADE (WITH A GROWN-UP'S SUPERVISION), CUT AIR VENTS IN THE SIDES OF YOUR BOX SO YOUR ROCK CAN BREATH.

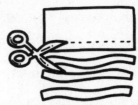

2 CUT THE CREPE PAPER IN NARROW STRIPS AND CRINKLE THEM INTO YOUR HANDS. SPRINKLE THEM ACROSS THE BOTTOM OF YOUR BOX.

(CONTINUED)

3. WRITE "MY ROCK PET" ON THE SIDE OF YOUR BOX.

4. FIND THE PERFECT ROCK AND SET IT INSIDE. DON'T FORGET TO FEED, WATER, AND TAKE YOUR ROCK OUT FOR WALKS.

5. EXTRA CREDIT: MAKE A MANUAL FOR YOUR ROCK WITH INSTRUCTIONS FOR ITS CARE.

We need to understand our past to protect our future. Today's paleontologists, like Stephen J. Gould, are still filling in the blanks of our civilization, discovering fossils like those in Colorado. Paleobotanists focus on plant life and how it evolved. They've shown how ferns first appeared after the meteor that wiped out the dinosaurs and how those eventually developed into forests. Geologists find rocks and minerals in the earth and figure out how to mine them for things we all use, like copper wiring and coal. They work to find natural resources, like oil and natural gas, which are used to make the electricity that powers our world. They also play an important role in protecting our planet from pollution and other threats to the environment. They examine air, dirt, water, or other substances to determine if the area is healthy and unpolluted. The human story would be incomplete without a full understanding of life on Earth.

Remember, too, the earth itself is a rock, and it's our job to protect it.

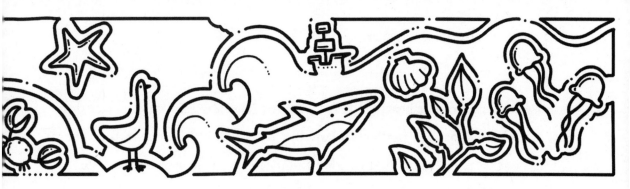

THE BEACH

CHAPTER TWO

I was visiting my grandparents in West Chop, Massachusetts, when Hurricane Carol hit. It was 1954, and I was seven years old. I was too young to be scared. Excited is more like it, as I watched my grandpa nail the French doors down to keep the storm from getting in. Our house was far enough back from the beach that we didn't have to worry about the huge waves reaching us, but other families had to evacuate the area. The storm was that strong. My mother was worried about two tiny beach cottages close to the water. The families were supposed to evacuate, and we didn't know if they had.

The next day, we went to investigate. I wore my yellow raincoat to go outside. Seven-foot waves had deposited giant pieces of seaweed halfway up our lawn. They glistened in the sun like a bed of emeralds. I can still remember stepping carefully over downed power wires that looked like snakes in the road. The ocean was at low tide, and the storm had left lots of shells and horseshoe crabs on the beach. When we came to the houses, it was the weirdest thing. One house was perfectly okay. But the picture window in the other was smashed, and water had flooded the place up to the ceiling. At seven, I didn't yet understand how storms gather in the middle of the ocean or their destructive power.

Hurricanes are also called typhoons and cyclones, but their scientific name is "tropical cyclones" because they form over oceans in warm waters. The moist air rises, and pressure builds beneath it. As it rises, warm air gathers around it and starts to spin as the pressure changes. You have probably heard about the "eye" of the storm. This is caused by high air pressure above the hurricane cloud pressing down from the top. The eye remains calm. Think of the white tube inside a huge gob of cotton candy. As hurricanes get closer to land, they lose their power, no longer fueled by the ocean's warm air. But even so, winds can reach speeds of over 130 miles per hour, and waves can be over twelve feet tall. Hurricane Carol was the worst storm to hit New England in nearly twenty years and caused massive damage.

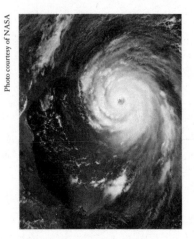

Photo courtesy of NASA

A satellite photo of a hurricane.

The West Chop peninsula stretches for six miles. It is surrounded almost completely by water and was fantastic for shell hunting. In New England, most shells come from mollusks, which include snails, mussels, clams, and oysters, among other species. Mollusk shells grow to protect the animal by forming a fleshy, skin-like substance that hardens and becomes part of the animal's body wall. It's called the mantle and produces calcium carbonate, a mineral found in baking powder and chalk, that bonds with a small amount of protein to form a hard shell. When a mollusk dies, its shell continues to exist.

One of my favorite kind of shells to collect were jingle shells, also known as mermaid's toenails. They're named for the sound they make when you shake a few in your hand, and also because they look like painted toenails. The shells are about one to two inches wide, though you can find ones as tiny as baby teeth. The ones I collected were generally orange in color, but they can also be white, yellow, or pink. They are paper thin (though strong) and have a pearly coat with iridescence, which is when colors change in the light, like the rainbow you sometimes see in a soap bubble or the blue-and-green shimmer in a peacock feather. Jingle shells are great for making wind chimes, jewelry, and mosaics.

PROJECT # 1
—— SEASHELL WIND CHIMES ——

You'll need:

- Ruler or tape measure
- Twine (You can use dental floss or heavy-duty thread in a pinch.)
- Scissors
- Hot glue gun
- Piece of wood several inches long (If you live near the beach, see if you can find a piece of driftwood, but a branch or dowel will also work.)
- About 25 seashells

Tip: It's easy if you collect seashells with holes. Holes are made when mollusks use something called a radula, which is like a tongue with tiny teeth to drill a hole into another shell to suck out the food. If you use seashells you collected from the beach, wash them thoroughly with soap and warm water to make sure you get rid of any unwanted bacteria that may be on the shells. If you can't get to a beach, many crafts stores sell seashells.

INSTRUCTIONS

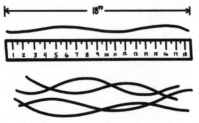

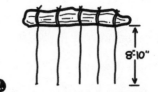

1. USING YOUR RULER OR TAPE MEASURE, MEASURE OUT FIVE PIECES OF TWINE 18 INCHES LONG AND CUT THEM WITH YOUR SCISSORS.

2. TIGHTLY TIE EACH STRAND OF TWINE TO YOUR PIECE OF WOOD, SPREAD OUT EVENLY, LEAVING ROUGHLY 8-10 INCHES DANGLING TO ATTACH YOUR SEASHELL CHIMES.

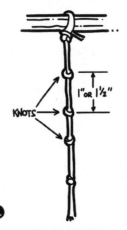

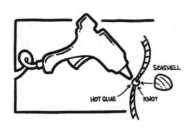

3. MAKE KNOTS EVERY INCH OR INCH AND A HALF ON YOUR TWINE. THESE KNOTS ARE WHERE YOU'LL GLUE THE SHELLS.

4. USING A HOT GLUE GUN, ATTACH THE SHELLS TO THE KNOTS.

5. CUT ANOTHER STRAND OF TWINE, ABOUT 12 INCHES LONG. TIE EACH END OF THE TWINE TO THE ENDS OF YOUR STICK, AND USE THIS TO HANG YOUR CHIMES.

PROJECT #2
SEASHELL NECKLACE

You'll need:

- Scissors
- String or thread (thin enough to fit through a hole made by a pushpin)
- Pushpin
- Seashells
- Beads, buttons, or any other materials you might want to add to your necklace

Tip: If you use seashells you collected from the beach, wash them thoroughly with soap and warm water to make sure you get rid of any unwanted bacteria that may be on the shells. If you can't get to a beach, many crafts stores sell seashells.

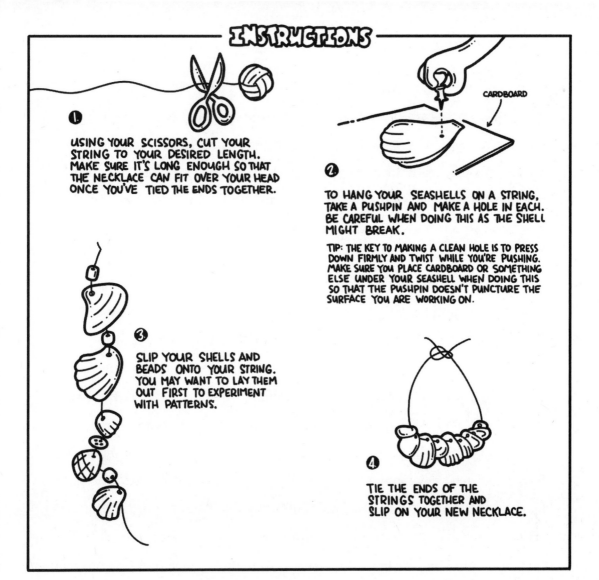

1. USING YOUR SCISSORS, CUT YOUR STRING TO YOUR DESIRED LENGTH. MAKE SURE IT'S LONG ENOUGH SO THAT THE NECKLACE CAN FIT OVER YOUR HEAD ONCE YOU'VE TIED THE ENDS TOGETHER.

CARDBOARD

2. TO HANG YOUR SEASHELLS ON A STRING, TAKE A PUSHPIN AND MAKE A HOLE IN EACH. BE CAREFUL WHEN DOING THIS AS THE SHELL MIGHT BREAK.

TIP: THE KEY TO MAKING A CLEAN HOLE IS TO PRESS DOWN FIRMLY AND TWIST WHILE YOU'RE PUSHING. MAKE SURE YOU PLACE CARDBOARD OR SOMETHING ELSE UNDER YOUR SEASHELL WHEN DOING THIS SO THAT THE PUSHPIN DOESN'T PUNCTURE THE SURFACE YOU ARE WORKING ON.

3. SLIP YOUR SHELLS AND BEADS ONTO YOUR STRING. YOU MAY WANT TO LAY THEM OUT FIRST TO EXPERIMENT WITH PATTERNS.

4. TIE THE ENDS OF THE STRINGS TOGETHER AND SLIP ON YOUR NEW NECKLACE.

Above all, my favorite beach activity was building sandcastles with my sister. Sand forms when rocks break down over millions of years and are worn away by the ocean's currents. At a distance, sand usually looks like it's one color, but on closer inspection, you'll also find broken-up seashells and coral. In New England, the beaches are mostly made of granite, which is why the sand there has a tan appearance, but it also has quartz, mica, feldspar, and other minerals and shells mixed in.

At the beach, I was the dribble expert, dribbling sand between my fingers to decorate our castles. I would get hypnotized doing this. Some people with autism, like me, really like doing things with repetitive motion. It can calm their nerves. That was probably true for me, but it was also about building these great structures with my sister. Long before I was designing cattle equipment, I was laying out the castles on a blueprint I drew with a stick in the sand. My sister and I had a method that started with getting the cornerstones in place, then building up the walls between them. We'd fill pails with sand that we mixed with ocean water. We understood through some trial and error that getting the water/sand consistency right is key to building sandcastles. According to an article in *NASA Science* called "The Physics of Science," sand sticks together due to tiny water bridges that form between the grains.

After packing the pail with our mixture, my sister would dump it upside down. The goal was having the form be as perfect as possible with no holes or cracks. My sister did most of the building while I did the dribble decorations. For dribbles, the best ratio is almost equal parts water to sand so that the sand is silky and watery. My goal was to make the dribbles resemble the stalagmites in caves. We would make turrets and moats that filled with sea-water as the tide came in and then emptied back out to the ocean as the tide went out. I could spend hours decorating the walls my sister built. I was very upset the first time the waves washed away our castle, but as I grew older, I kind of liked knowing they would return to the ocean.

Temple Grandin Archive

If you look closely, you can see my sand dribbles on the castle walls.

SANDCASTLES

You'll need:

- Sand (If you don't live near a beach, you can use a sandbox or a plastic tub or bin and fill it with sand, which you can find at a local hardware store. Please do not bring this into the house, unless an adult says it's okay.)
- Water

- Pail (Multiple pails of different sizes are also good, but you can improvise with Dixie cups, coffee cans, or any carton.)
- Shells, pebbles, sticks, seaweed (optional)

INSTRUCTIONS

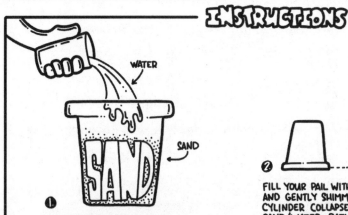

WATER

SAND

❶ BRING YOUR SAND TO THE RIGHT CONSISTENCY BY SLOWLY ADDING WATER. YOU CAN ALWAYS ADD MORE WATER.

❷ FILL YOUR PAIL WITH WET SAND, TURN IT OVER, AND GENTLY SHIMMY THE PAIL OFF. IF YOUR SAND CYLINDER COLLAPSES, EXPERIMENT WITH THE SAND/WATER RATIO AND HOW TIGHTLY YOU PACK THE SAND INTO THE PAIL.

❸ ONCE YOU'VE CREATED YOUR STRUCTURE THE REAL FUN BEGINS: DRIBBLE DECORATIONS BY LOOSELY HOLDING THE WET SAND IN YOUR HAND WITH YOUR PALM FACEDOWN LIKE A CLAW. LET THE WATERY SAND SLOWLY DRIBBLE DOWN LIKE SAND IN AN HOURGLASS ONTO THE TOP OF YOUR CASTLE.

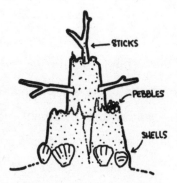

STICKS

PEBBLES

SHELLS

❹ YOU CAN ALSO DECORATE WITH SHELLS, PEBBLES, STICKS, AND SEAWEED.

THE SILENT WORLD

One of the most well-known undersea explorers was a man named Jacques Cousteau. He filmed whales and shark feeding frenzies and fish that looked like they were a million years old. He got up close to schools of brightly colored fish that swam in patterns and to reefs of colored coral that looked like brains or underwater forests. He himself said that his films weren't documentaries; they were adventures. The motto on his ship the *Calypso* was "We must go and see for ourselves."

Jacques's first love was flying, and he was training to be a pilot when he broke both his arms in a car accident. It was through swimming that he healed and gained back his strength. That experience with the ocean changed the direction of his life. Later he would write, "I loved touching water. . . . Water fascinated me."

Jacques had another love as well: filming. He got his first camera at age thirteen, and he took it apart and put it together before shooting a single frame. Eventually, he would bring these two passions together, capturing the mysteries of the sea in his first film, *The Silent World*.

But he would need something else to fulfill his dreams. Divers had been using something called a diving bell to go underwater, and it was extremely heavy and severely limited the diver's movement and ability to see. Jacques invented a lightweight apparatus to help him breathe underwater for longer periods of time and allow him to swim with more flexibility. His invention, the "Aqua-Lung," consisted of an air tank and a tube that brought the air from the tank to the diver's mouth, which later became known as scuba (which stands for "self-contained underwater breathing apparatus"). But the key innovation was the regulator, which adjusted the air pressure, depending on the depth of the water. Near the end of his life, Jacques said that he could fly in any direction when he was underwater. It struck me that he fulfilled his dream of flying after all.

A crane lifts Cousteau's diving saucer.

I was endlessly fascinated by all the things I found just walking along the shore. One of my most exciting finds was a propane cylinder that had washed up on the beach. My sister and I were afraid it might be dangerous, so we didn't lug it home. I couldn't imagine where it came from. My other most exciting find became a prized possession: a seagull garden ornament with propellers for wings. It was in great shape and I carted it home to my garage to keep with all my special finds.

More common finds were seaweed, sea glass, shells, horseshoe crabs, driftwood, and starfish. I'd make projects out of them when I got back to the house. Seaweed was tricky because I needed to cart it home in seawater or it would dry up. My mother wasn't happy about having a pail of seaweed sloshing all over the back of her car. That's when I came up with coffee cans as a means of transport, because they have lids. Seaweed, which is technically an alga and not a weed, can be minuscule or grow to 100 feet in length. It plays a hugely important role to both fish and humans. For fish, it provides a virtual buffet, trapping the little critters that live in the crevices of the seaweed. For humans, seaweed performs another critical function in the ecosystem by producing 70 percent of the air that we breathe using photosynthesis, the process by which plants convert carbon dioxide into oxygen. As a kid, I loved pressing seaweed the way we pressed flowers. Some of my favorite kinds of seaweed were "dead man's hands," "sea lettuce," and "mermaid's hair."

Wikimedia Commons/B.navez

This is the kind of seaweed I used to mount on cardboard. The thinner the fronds the better.

PROJECT # 4
PRESSED SEAWEED ART

You'll need:

- Seaweed
- Ocean water
- Container with a lid (like a coffee can or Tupperware)
- Shallow tray

- Tap water
- Watercolor paper or blotter paper
- Corrugated cardboard
- Mesh fabric
- 2 heavy books

Tip: *There are some seaweeds that are very thin and will cling tightly to the cardboard. If these seaweeds are used, pressing with books may not be required.*

INSTRUCTIONS

1. VISIT A BEACH AND LOOK IN THE SHALLOW WATER FOR ANY SEAWEED – YOU WANT TO FIND SEAWEED WITH THE THINNEST FRONDS. MY FAVORITE SPECIES TO USE IS *ULVA LINZA*, WHICH IS LIKE RUBBERY CREPE PAPER, BUT YOU CAN FOLLOW YOUR OWN IDEAS AND PREFERENCES. COLLECT SPECIMENS TO BRING HOME. (IF YOU DON'T LIVE NEAR AN OCEAN, EXPERIMENT WITH YARN, CREPE PAPER, OR EVEN RUBBER BANDS, WHICH CAN BE CUT IN HALF TO LOOK LIKE SEAWEED FRONDS. EXPERIMENT WITH ANYTHING WAVY.)

2. TRANSPORT YOUR SEAWEED WITH A SMALL AMOUNT OF OCEAN WATER IN A CONTAINER WITH A TOP TO KEEP FROM SPILLING.

③ ONCE HOME, FILL A SHALLOW TRAY OR PAN WITH ABOUT TWO INCHES OF TAP WATER AND PLACE YOUR SEAWEED SPECIMENS INSIDE.

④ SLIDE THE SHEET OF WATERCOLOR PAPER UNDER THE SEAWEED IN THE TRAY SO THAT THE PAPER IS COMPLETELY SUBMERGED.

⑤ USING YOUR FINGERS, SHAPE THE SEAWEED INTO WHATEVER DESIGN YOU WANT. BE SURE THE SEAWEED ISN'T LAYERED TOO THICK ON ANY PART OF THE PAPER OR ELSE IT MAY COME OUT LOOKING LUMPY.

⑥ CAREFULLY LIFT THE PAPER WITH THE SEAWEED ON TOP FROM THE TRAY, GENTLY TIPPING THE SHEET TO LET THE WATER RUN OFF WITHOUT LOSING YOUR DESIGN.

CARDBOARD

⑦ PLACE THE SHEET ON A PIECE OF CARDBOARD. IF YOUR DESIGN SHIFTED WHILE LIFTING THE SHEET OUT OF THE WATER, READJUST IT NOW.

← ANOTHER PIECE OF CARDBOARD

← MESH FABRIC

⑧ LAY THE MESH FABRIC OVER YOUR ART AND ANOTHER LAYER OF CARDBOARD ON TOP OF THAT.

⑨ PLACE A FEW HEAVY BOOKS ON TOP TO PRESS DOWN ON THE ART.

⑩ AFTER ABOUT THREE DAYS, LIFT THE BOOKS AND MESH OFF AND TAKE A LOOK AT YOUR ART. IF THE SEAWEED AND PAPER STILL AREN'T DRY, YOU'LL WANT TO PLACE THEM BACK UNDER THE BOOKS AND WAIT A LITTLE LONGER. IF THEY'RE DRY, THEN YOU'RE READY TO FRAME AND HANG UP YOUR ART!

Sea glass was pure treasure. I loved hunting for it up and down the beach. Sea glass comes from . . . glass. Pretty much any glass that gets dumped into the ocean will break down and become sea glass. Most sea glass you find on the beach comes from shards of glass bottles discarded in the ocean, which explains why the most common colors are white, green, and brown. Sea glass comes in lots of other colors, but those specimens are more difficult to find: orange, yellow, pink, and turquoise. The shards could come from any glass object, such as a vase, lamp, or perfume bottle. It's possible that a piece of sea glass on a Massachusetts beach could have come from a goblet on an eighteenth-century ship.

All sea glass is created by the ocean's currents, which smooth its edges, sometimes for as long as centuries. Some pieces have a frosted appearance or cloudy film, which comes from the salt in the ocean water. Sea glass keeps its color even after hundreds of years; if you toss a green bottle into the ocean, it will one day wash ashore as green sea glass.

Unfortunately, lots of trash and plastic are being thrown into the sea, and it is harming fish and other sea animals. Plastic is a serious problem. Sea birds, marine animals, and fish can starve to death when they mistake plastic for particles for food, clogging up their digestive tract.

Another problem is called microplastics. They are tiny bits of plastic that are created when plastic bottles and other items break apart. Some plastics float, and they have created gyres, or floating rafts of plastic trash. The biggest offenders for creating "garbage patches" are floating plastic fishing nets that have been lost by fishermen. This plastic pollution can last for years because many plastics are stable and do not degrade. Everybody needs to stop throwing plastic into the ocean.

You can make lots of projects with sea glass. My favorite was a turtle

I made with a jingle shell for the body and sea glass for the head and arms and legs. But you can design almost anything with sea glass: mosaics, boxes, jewelry, frames, and sculptures.

PROJECT #5
SEA GLASS AND SHELL TURTLE

You'll need:

- Cardboard or plywood
- Sea glass (If you don't live near a beach, you can purchase sea glass at a local crafts store or find inexpensive bags online, though these are usually machine made.)

- Cockle shell or clamshell
- Superglue or epoxy
- Paint
- Paintbrush

INSTRUCTIONS

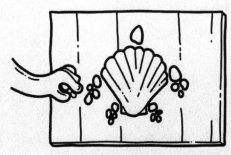

1 ON THE CARDBOARD OR PLYWOOD, ARRANGE YOUR PIECES OF SEA GLASS AROUND YOUR SHELL TO CREATE A ROUND HEAD AND FIN-SHAPED LEGS. (YOU CAN USE ONE SHELL FOR EACH OF THESE OR PUT A FEW TOGETHER TO MAKE THE RIGHT SHAPE.)

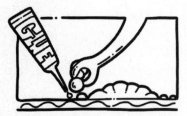

2 GLUE THE PIECES IN YOUR DESIGN ONTO THE CARDBOARD OR PLYWOOD.

(CONTINUED)

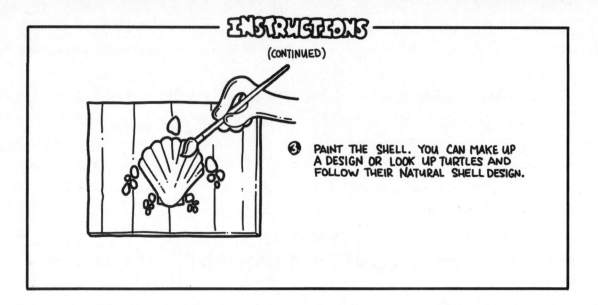

INSTRUCTIONS

(CONTINUED)

③ PAINT THE SHELL. YOU CAN MAKE UP A DESIGN OR LOOK UP TURTLES AND FOLLOW THEIR NATURAL SHELL DESIGN.

Driftwood always looks a bit otherworldly when you come across it, like it belongs in a desert instead of by the ocean. When I was very young, I had read that driftwood could come from sunken pirate ships, which motivated me to find as many pieces as possible. Driftwood is basically any wooden plank, branch, log, or tree trunk that ends up in a body of water, either from natural causes, like storms, or man-made activities, like logging. Like sea glass, the wood is worn smooth by the waves and sand. Sometimes we'd find a piece with branches still sticking out that looked like antlers. I also observed little bugs hiding in the nooks and crannies of the wood. Even though wood that washes up on shore is technically dead, it is still part of the ecological cycle.

There are lots of projects you can make with a piece of driftwood, depending on the shape you find. Let the wood inspire you! I enjoyed gluing rocks to driftwood and painting them to look like birds on a wire. Other ideas include frames and wreaths.

Sometimes driftwood looks like sculpture.

DRIFTWOOD WREATH

- Newspaper
- Medium-sized plate
- Lots of pieces of driftwood
  (You can cut them into the same
  size or use them at their natural
  lengths. If you don't live near a
  beach, you can substitute with
  twigs.)

- Glue
- Ribbon, jingle shells, colored
  yarn, bows (optional)
- Scissors
- Twine

INSTRUCTIONS

1. SPREAD OUT NEWSPAPER TO KEEP THE TABLE FROM BECOMING A GLUEY MESS. USE THE PLATE TO MARK THE CENTER OF THE WREATH.

2. ARRANGE THE PIECES OF DRIFTWOOD AROUND THE PLATE SO THEY'RE TOUCHING ONE ANOTHER TO MAKE A CIRCLE, THEN GLUE THEM TOGETHER TO MAKE YOUR BASE.

3. REMOVE THE PLATE, THEN LAYER THE PIECES OF WOOD ON THE BASE, AND BUILD OUT TO MAKE A LARGER WREATH.

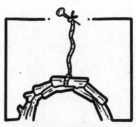

5. CUT A LENGTH OF TWINE (YOU CAN MAKE IT AS LONG AS YOU NEED DEPENDING ON WHERE YOU PLAN TO HANG YOUR WREATH) AND THREAD IT THROUGH THE TOP OF YOUR WREATH. TIE A KNOT AT THE TOP.

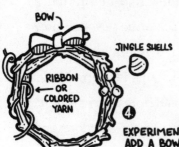

BOW

JINGLE SHELLS

RIBBON OR COLORED YARN

4. EXPERIMENT WITH DECORATIONS: ADD A BOW, GLUE JINGLE SHELLS, OR THREAD RIBBON OR COLORED YARN THROUGH THE SPACES BETWEEN THE TWIGS.

UNDER THE SEA

As a child, Robert Ballard was so taken with Jules Verne's science-fiction classic *Twenty Thousand Leagues Under the Sea,* about a marine biologist who fights an underwater sea creature, that it fueled his passion to become a naval intelligence officer and oceanographer. He never veered from his vision. His interests were also influenced by growing up along the coast of California, where he was fascinated by the sea creatures that he encountered while snorkeling and swimming. "As a child I was always curious about things and I was fortunate enough not to have that passion extinguished as I grew up," Ballard once said.

Ballard is known for two extraordinary discoveries. The first has to do with finding life on the ocean floor. Scientists initially believed that the ocean floor was too dark and cold to support life. In 1977, Ballard and his team, using a remote-controlled submersible camera, were able to explore the ocean floor, where they discovered "hypothermic vents" that let out dark plumes of nearly boiling water called "black smokers." They found what are called "giant tube worms" near the hypothermic vents that do not need sunlight, instead relying on bacteria in their own bodies to survive. Ballard had discovered a whole ecosystem that no one knew existed. Scientific research now shows that the metabolism of the two worms is totally different compared to most animals. They are almost like an alien form of life.

His other discovery involves a ship that set sail from Southampton, England, to New York City in 1912. The ship was over 882 feet long and weighed 46,328 tons. It was the world's largest ship at the time of its first and only voyage, and it carried some of the wealthiest people in the world. The ship was equipped with a gymnasium, pool, libraries, ballrooms, restaurants, and elegant sleeping cabins. You've probably already guessed its name: the *Titanic*. More than 1,500 people died when it sank in the middle of the North Atlantic Ocean, and it was rumored to have over seven million dollars' worth of diamonds in its safe. Though many tried to find the sunken ship over the decades, none were successful until Ballard. Aided by sonar mapping, livestreams from submersible cameras that are viewed on computer monitors, and undersea robots, Ballard and his crew found the famous boat seventy-three years after it sank to 12,000 feet below the sea.

To this day, Ballard continues his scientific work exploring the sea floor in *Nautilus*, an exploration vessel named after Captain Nemo's ship in *Twenty Thousand Leagues Under the Sea*. His mission is also to educate the next generation of oceanographers. The first line of Ballard's book *The Eternal Darkness* is something I deeply believe in: "All of us are born explorers."

At the beach, I could observe for what seemed like hours the graceful way jellyfish drifted through the water, expanding and collapsing as they moved. Most have a bell shape with long stringy tentacles that trail behind them like hair as they swim. They sail along the ocean's currents the way parachutes sail through the air. We'd often come across them while hunting for sea treasure. Most look harmless enough, like clear blobs of jelly or polliwogs (another name for tadpoles). My fascination with jellyfish ended one summer day when a really nasty boy put a jellyfish in my root beer. It tasted horrible and I spit it out just in time, before the ball of slime went down my throat. It was one of the worst tricks anyone ever tried to play on me.

This is the kind of jellyfish I used to see on Martha's Vineyard.

Wikimedia Commons/Dan90266

Photo courtesy of the U.S. Department of Defense

Parachutes remind me of the graceful way jellyfish propel through the ocean.

When jellyfish aren't being used to gross you out, though, they are scientifically impressive. For starters, they have been around for over 500 million years. They don't have brains, hearts, or bones, and their bodies are 96 percent water (in comparison, humans contain up to 60 percent water), but they are extremely efficient. A hole in their underside both eats foods and gets rid of waste. Make no mistake, some jellyfish can be dangerous, such as the box jellyfish in Australia. They kill more people than sharks. They have venom-stinging cells that, like microscopic harpoons, pierce your skin. In the United States, the Portuguese man-of-war is less dangerous, but it is still hazardous. Instead of swimming underwater like most jellyfish, its tentacles float beneath an air-filled sack. It may look like a partially inflated plastic bag.

If you get stung by a jellyfish, first, you'll feel a tingling feeling; then the sting will start to hurt, and your arm or leg could go completely numb. Those venomous stingers are meant for paralyzing prey, like fish and shrimp. There is an old wives' tale (which means a story with *no* basis in scientific facts) that your own pee is the best cure for jellyfish stings. This is incorrect. Vinegar rinse or ocean water is the best medicine.

UNDER THE SEA WIND

In an introduction to the 1994 edition of *Silent Spring*, Rachel Carson's groundbreaking book on the environment, Vice President Al Gore wrote that she was one of the reasons he became so passionate about protecting the earth. "Her picture hangs on my office wall among those of political leaders. . . . Carson has had as much or more effect on me than any of them, and perhaps more than all of them together." *Silent Spring* alerted people to the damage pesticides were doing to our food and world. It also started the global movement of environmentalism. We hear a lot about these issues today, but Carson was a true pioneer, educating people about the fact that humans need to change how we treat the environment or risk losing it.

But her first love was the ocean. According to her biographer, Linda Lear, Carson found a large fossilized shell as a girl. But finding it wasn't enough; it sparked a bunch of questions. Where did it come from? What animal made it or lived in it? Later, Carson would say she had an "absolute fascination for everything relating to the ocean." She also loved writing from a young age and published her first story in a children's magazine when she was ten years old. Later, after she graduated college with a degree in zoology, she began working as a biologist for the U.S. Bureau of Fisheries, where she started publishing articles about the ocean. She would bring this experience to *Under the Sea-Wind*, the first of her trio of books on the ocean. "No matter how hard the wind might be blowing, Carson walked the beach at all hours," wrote Lear. "Sometimes she simply lay in the sandy dunes, flat on her back, arms behind her head, watching and listening to the birds as they circled and dived overhead." Carson's favorite thing to do was take night walks on the beach with her flashlight, looking for all sorts of nocturnal critters unseen during the day, taking notes in her little black notebook, recording all the night smells, sounds, and sights. Carson herself sums it up best: "In every curving beach, in every grain of sand, there is a story of the earth."

Carson and a fellow marine biologist in the field.

Photo courtesy of the U.S. Fish and Wildlife Service

Our family went to Martha's Vineyard during the summer via ferry. For me it was sort of excruciating because of the sound of the horn. Many autistic people have sensitivities to sound, and it was a real problem for me. A dentist drill sounded like a jackhammer. And the horn on the ferry was deafening. Mother would let me go down below deck, where I'd find a corner and plug my ears as hard as I could. Once I got through that, I loved all the different kinds of things we did on the beach on the Vineyard. The town where we stayed, West Chop, had a pier where we fished for flounder. The beach there was calm, and I remember collecting lots of starfish, though their more accurate name is "sea star."

This is the kind of starfish I used to find on Cape Cod and Martha's Vineyard.

Turns out starfish aren't fish at all. They are invertebrates, which means they don't have a backbone. They more closely resemble sand dollars and sea urchins than fish. When you find them on the beach and they are dried, it's fine to pick them up and take them home. But if they are wet, they are still alive, and you do not want to touch them. Like jellyfish, they also release venom.

Sea stars usually have five points, though some can grow as many as fifty arms. A sea star generally looks harmless enough and pretty, but they are fierce. They protect themselves from predators with their hard, scaly skin, and most remarkably, if a predator should bite off a limb, the sea star can grow it back, or regenerate. Scientists have been attempting to unlock the mystery of regeneration since the early 1700s. As humans, our hair and nails grow back; imagine if we could grow back a limb or organ.

Sea stars also have bizarre table manners. Instead of putting food in their mouths and swallowing like we do, so that the food is transported to the stomach for digestion, they literally put their stomachs on their food. A sea star will use its arms to wrench open the shell of a mollusk, then stick its stomach out of its mouth into the mollusk's shell. Acid from the sea star's stomach breaks down the mollusk, making it easier to digest when the sea star retracts its stomach back into its body. As if that wasn't strange enough, sea stars have eyes at the ends of their arms that detect changes in light intensity, essentially "seeing" with their arms.

PROJECT # 7
STARFISH DECORATION

You'll need:

- Pushpin
- Starfish (If you don't have a beach nearby to collect starfish, you can purchase them at a local crafts store. You can also make your own using the dough recipe from the fossil project on page 23.)
- Newspaper
- Spray paint or paint and paintbrush
- Glue
- Decorations: sequins, baby pearls, glitter
- Sewing needle with large eye
- ¼" ribbon

INSTRUCTIONS

1. USING A PUSHPIN, GENTLY PUNCTURE THE END OF THE STARFISH'S ARM, ROTATING THE PIN UNTIL IT GOES THROUGH.

2. SPREAD OUT NEWSPAPER AND SPRAY-PAINT OR PAINT YOUR STARFISH. LET IT DRY.

3. COVER YOUR STARFISH WITH A LAYER OF GLUE.

④ DECORATE YOUR STARFISH WITH BEADS, GLITTER, ETC. LET IT DRY.

⑤

AS WITH SEWING, THREAD THE RIBBON THROUGH THE EYE OF THE NEEDLE AND GUIDE IT THROUGH THE HOLE, THEN TIE THE ENDS OF THE STRING TOGETHER. (THE LENGTH OF THE RIBBON CAN BE AS SHORT OR AS LONG AS YOU LIKE.) YOU'RE READY TO HANG IT IN A WINDOW OR ON A WALL, OR WRAP IT AS A PRESENT.

Just as starfish aren't fish, horseshoe crabs aren't crabs. Genetically, they have more in common with scorpions and spiders. I first came upon a whole lot of horseshoe crabs in the harbor mudflats in West Chop after Hurricane Carol. I thought they looked prehistoric, which makes sense since they've been around for over 400 million years; they existed 200 million years earlier than the dinosaurs did. The horseshoe crabs we see today look pretty much the same as they did 400 million years ago. We know this because of the fossil record.

Horseshoe crabs are named for U-shaped horseshoes. But they always looked more like helmets to me. In fact, when I once tried to put one on my head, my mother scolded me, claiming they were filled with bacteria, and I never did it again. Horseshoe crabs "molt" their helmets, meaning they shed them and grow new ones (the way snakes shed their skin) about sixteen times until they are full adults (which is when they are about ten years old).

The horseshoe crab's body has three sections: head, abdomen, and tail. Most people think that the sharp, pointy tail is a poisonous stinger. The tail's job is to turn the crab right side up if it gets stuck on its back. It digs into the

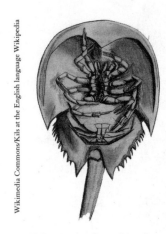

I always turned over horseshoe crabs to investigate what was underneath their hard shell.

sand and works like a lever to flip the crab back over. We used to pick up the crabs by their tails and watch their gills flap before throwing them back in the ocean. Like the sea star, the horseshoe crab has a strange way of eating. It doesn't have any teeth, so instead it uses two of its ten legs to crush food (worms, clams, and algae) before putting it in its mouth. Horseshoe crabs also have nine eyes and can see both regular light and ultraviolet light, helping them avoid predators, such as birds, reptiles, and fish.

My favorite activity on the Vineyard was going to the big pier at West Chop and zooming down a riptide channel. A riptide or rip current runs perpendicular to the waves, and unlike the waves, it is beneath the ocean's surface and you can't see it. Someone at the pier had attached two long, thick ropes, sort of like the lane dividers in a swimming pool, from the pier to a floating raft. The raft was made of fifty-five-gallon oil drums, with a ladder attached to pull yourself up out of the water. You would hold on to the ropes with all your strength as the riptide forced you down the channel to the raft. The current did the work, but you had to hold on to those ropes for dear life. The whole thing only took about ten seconds, but it was better than any amusement park ride, and I would do it four or five times until I was entirely exhausted. Swimming in the rip current without the ropes would have been really dangerous. According to the United States Lifesaving Association (USLA.org), rip currents are the leading hazards at surf beaches.

Once, when my siblings and I were coasting on the waves, our bodies bouncing up and down like corks, I suddenly got pulled farther and farther out to sea. The waves were high that day, all the more fun to jump, but I had no idea that the strong current of a riptide was running beneath us. Before I knew it, the current had pulled me far out. I was about eight or nine and it was terrifying. Thank goodness a man on the beach realized what was going on when he saw how far I had gotten. He must have known it was a rip current pulling me because instead of diving in to get me, he ran farther down the beach, parallel to the water, to get ahead of the current and intercept me. When my mother realized what happened, she was alternately freaking out and thanking the man. We never even found out who he was. Just a good person.

IN WHAT ENDED UP BEING A LARGE-SCALE CURRENT PROJECT, a shipping crate filled with 29,000 plastic yellow duckies, green frogs, red beavers, and blue turtles accidentally fell overboard somewhere between Hong Kong and the United States in 1992. That may sound unusual, but shipping containers on ships have a bad habit of falling off during storms. Some of these will sink to the bottom of the ocean, but when they are filled with things that are packaged in Styrofoam, they float. These steel containers bobbing on the ocean surface are also known as "steel icebergs" and are very dangerous to boats and ships. Only two years before the rubber ducky incident, 61,000 pairs of Nike running shoes fell off a ship.

What at first seemed like a ducky disaster turned into a global science experiment as people all over the world, a network of volunteers, combed beaches for the bath toys and running shoes to report their finds, discovering huge ocean currents and their patterns. This effort was headed up by oceanographer Dr. Curtis Ebbesmeyer. The toys first started washing ashore in Alaska, then in Japan, and then, surprisingly, back in Alaska again after about two years and 4,600 miles. Ebbesmeyer continued to track the ducks and the Nike shoes as they landed in Seattle, China, and the Arctic for over twenty years. He was able to show that ocean currents known as gyres, which are massive interlocking currents, circle the earth. "There's a lot of scientific information just lying on the beach," Ebbesmeyer said.

One of the rubber duckies that washed up on the beach after the shipping container spill.

PROJECT # 8
NURDLE HUNTING

In 2018, a nurdle spill turned up along the Texas coastline. A nurdle sounds like something out of a Dr. Seuss book, but it's a small plastic pellet the size of a lentil and is used as the raw material in almost everything plastic. They come in lots of colors. In Texas, a team of volunteers removed 230,000 nurdles.

Nurdles get spread around when they spill from trucks and at sea. Besides polluting the environment, the nurdles can be ingested by fish and wildlife.

A "nurdle" is a funny word for a plastic resin pellet that often winds up as debris on our beautiful beaches.

You'll need:

- Paper
- Pencil
- Beach
- Container

- Magnifying glass (optional)
- Nurdle ID sheet:
  nurdlehunt.org.uk/images/Leaflets
  /Nurdles-ID-chart_final.pdf

INSTRUCTIONS

1. MAKE YOUR NURDLE RECORDING FORM. LIST NAME, LOCATION, DATE, STARTING TIME, ENDING TIME, TIME HUNTING, TOTAL NUMBER OF NURDLES FOUND, AND NOTES SUCH AS WEATHER, KIND OF BEACH (ROCY, SANDY), AND POLLUTION ON BEACH.

2. COLLECT AS MANY NURDLES AS YOU CAN. YOU DON'T HAVE TO USE A MAGNIFYING GLASS, BUT IF THE BEACH IS VERY PEBBLY IT MIGHT HELP TO SEE THEM.

3. SUBMIT YOUR REPORT TO Nurdlehunt.org.uk REPORT YOUR FINDINGS EVEN IF YOU DON'T FIND ANY! THAT'S ALSO IMPORTANT INFORMATION ABOUT THE ENVIRONMENT.

An old-fashioned way to track ocean currents is to send a message in a bottle, though people used to put messages in bottles for all kinds of reasons. Before communication on ships was possible, people left messages in bottles to say goodbye to loved ones, in the event that they became shipwrecked. Some messages were calls for help, some made confessions of crimes, and others were declarations of love. I was only interested in messages in bottles as a means of tracing currents and usually used a discarded bottle of my parents' wine that came packaged in a straw basket, which I figured would help it float. I'd write my message on typing paper, which was still legible even if it suffered a little water damage, asking the folks who'd find it to write to me and tell me where they found the bottle. I used the same cork it came with to plug it up and threw it either out into the ocean or off the Martha's Vineyard ferry. My siblings and I would just chuck them out and hope for the best. I probably sent out about twenty bottles and got responses to around half of them. The one that went the farthest got all the way to Maine! One time, I improvised with a pill bottle that I tied to a block of wood. It was successful and I received a letter. Sometimes improvising works. Even if it isn't successful, improvising is always worth a shot. That's how the best discoveries are sometimes made.

HER ROYAL DEEPNESS

Sylvia Earle had one dream: to touch the ocean floor. Others had done it, but she wanted to touch down without a tether to her vessel, which deep divers used in case of emergency. There was no aspect of ocean life that didn't fascinate Sylvia, and deep solo diving was her passion.

In 1979, Sylvia would achieve her dream. A tech wizard named Graham Hawkes had updated an old diving apparatus called a JIM suit. It looks something like an astronaut suit, has little claws on the ends of its arms to pick things up, and is big enough inside that the wearer can shift around and take notes inside the suit. Wearing the JIM suit, Sylvia was attached to the front of a small submersible and carried to the bottom of the ocean, where she then detached and explored the ocean floor off the coast of Hawaii. At 1,250 feet below the surface of the sea, it was the deepest ever untethered dive ever.

Years later, Sylvia and Graham designed a submersible called a Phantom that had a lightweight battery and was inexpensive to operate. It had manipulator arms and a suction device called a "slurp gun" for collecting and examining plants and animals. Sylvia said, "Like doctors who must first study human anatomy, we need to know how the earth and its oceans work when they're healthy so we can fix them when they're not." She also sized it up this way, which says it all: "There is life in every teaspoon of water."

Photo courtesy of NOAA

Sylvia Earle in her favorite place on Earth: deep beneath the sea. Here she displays marine samples to an aquanaut.

On a recent visit to the beach, I wound up getting upset. There was a lot of garbage and plastic all over the place. I saw fast food containers and plastic bottles from soda and Gatorade on the sand. Some people didn't pick up after their pets! I think people used to be more respectful of nature, but it's also true that we just didn't have as much garbage. We packed our own picnics, used plates and silverware, and cleaned up after ourselves. We mixed Kool-Aid in a thermos and returned our Coke bottles to the little general store for five cents (which we used to buy a Popsicle). We wouldn't dream of leaving trash on the beach. My mother always said, "Leave this place cleaner than you found it." I still think it is good advice. I meet a lot of young people at my talks, and I can tell they care a great deal about the environment, which gives me a lot of hope for the planet. There is nothing more beautiful than a pristine beach with pebbles and shells glistening in the surf and the vast ocean beyond.

THE WOODS

CHAPTER THREE

Growing up, I spent every minute that I could outside. Being inside meant being quiet. We had to use inside voices and mind our manners. When I chewed with my mouth open, my mother would tell me to chew with my mouth closed. My parents were also strict about chores. I was required to make my bed and keep my room tidy. For me, being inside also meant lots of extra schooling. Because of my autism, I didn't speak until I was four. I had a hard time focusing, and I was still a very poor reader at age eight.

When I was three, my mother hired a governess to help me stay "connected" to other people. She kept me from distractions and made sure I paid attention and always had good table manners. Everything my governess did with me, including playing games, was structured with a lot of emphasis on learning how to wait and take turns. We also spent lots of time outside building snowmen, sledding, and going for walks.

When I was eight and still not reading at grade level, my mother sat down and read a book with me every day after school, helping me sound out each word until I was reading on my own. I quickly advanced from the third-grade level to the sixth-grade level. I mention all this so that you will understand why I loved the outdoors so much. After a long day of school and then working on skills or drilling words with my mother, plus chores, getting to go outside meant one thing: FREEDOM!

We played in front of our house, the woods behind our house, and neighborhood streets where we raced our bikes and played tons of kick the can. But for me, the magic was in the woods at my elementary school, where kids gathered to play hide-and-seek during recess. Sometimes I'd find a ditch and cover myself with leaves as camouflage. One time, I stuffed a jacket and hat with leaves like a scarecrow and used it as a decoy so that the seeker would be thrown off course while I ran to home base. It was a thrill waiting to see if my spot would go undetected, holding my breath as the person searched through the woods, hearing their sneakers crunch the leaves.

The woods were my idea of a perfect playground. Sometimes, in the summer, my mother would let us camp out at the neighbors'. We spent hours putting up an old army tent. The parents never helped us. They let us do it ourselves. Another time we made elaborate tents from old sheets in our pine grove. We used twine to fasten the sheets to the trees and several spools of carpet thread to sew the sheets together. It was a lot of fun.

SHEET TENT

You'll need:

- 2 trees close together
- Scissors
- 2 old sheets or bedspreads
- Shoelaces
- Twine
- Chair or ladder
- 4 large rocks

INSTRUCTIONS

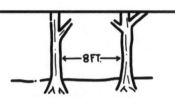

1. FIND TWO TREES THAT ARE CLOSE ENOUGH THAT YOU COULD HANG A HAMMOCK FROM THEM, ABOUT 8 FEET APART.

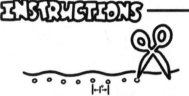

2. USE THE SCISSORS TO POKE HOLES ALONG THE LENGTH OF EACH SHEET, LEAVING AN INCH BETWEEN EACH HOLE.

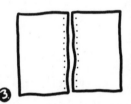

3. LINE UP BOTH SHEETS SO THAT THE HOLES ALIGNED.

4. TIE A KNOT IN ONE END OF A SHOELACE TO KEEP THE LACE FROM SLIDING OUT AND THREAD IT THROUGH THE HOLES OVER THE TOP OF THE SHEETS AND BACK AROUND. THIS IS KNOWN AS AN OVERCAST STITCH. AS YOU NEED MORE "ROPE," TIE MORE SHOELACES TOGETHER AND KEEP THREADING.

5. MEASURE OUT TWO LENGTHS OF TWINE TO CONNECT EACH END OF THE SHEETS TO THE TREES, WITH LOTS OF EXTRA TWINE TO WRAP AROUND THE TREE.

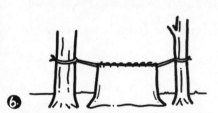

6. RUN THE TWINE FROM THE LAST HOLE IN THE SHEET TO THE TREE. YOU WILL PROBABLY NEED A LADDER OR A CHAIR TO TIE THE TWINE HIGH ENOUGH AROUND THE TREE SO THAT WHEN YOU'VE TIED THE SHEET END TO THE TREE, IT TOUCHES THE GROUND WITH A COUPLE OF INCHES TO SPARE.

7. PULL THE BOTTOM CORNERS OF THE SHEETS AWAY FROM EACH OTHER TO MAKE AN UPSIDE DOWN V SHAPE.

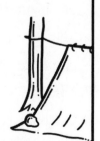

8. SECURE THE CORNERS OF THE SHEETS DOWN WITH ROCKS.

The outdoors was a natural playground. We spent hours searching for emerald moss, mica, rocks, and bird nests in our yard and our neighbors' yards up and down the street. We were taught never to disturb a nest that had either eggs or baby birds in it. Long before I knew what a botanist was (it's a person who studies plants), I was busy observing and sometimes taking apart every leaf and flower bed in the yard.

We'd identify animal tracks and amass hundreds of acorns for the Great Acorn War with the kids across the street. We'd spend whole afternoons hunting for four-leaf clovers because we believed they were lucky. I've since learned that the odds of finding a four-leaf clover are 10,000 to 1, which makes them really lucky and really rare. Technically, both three- and four-leaf clovers only have one leaf, made of three or four "leaflets." So, you're actually hunting for a four-leaflet clover. It's not exactly clear what causes the mutation in four-leaf clovers, but they are thought to be more common in warmer places, which may explain why we didn't have much luck finding them in New England. According to Guinness World Records, the most clover leaflets found on a single stem is fifty-six.

The trees in our yard were great for climbing. All you needed was a tree with a branch low enough to get a leg up. Neighborhood friends and I would take comic books, snacks, slingshots, flashlights, just about anything up in those trees. Sometimes we'd fashion a hook out of a hanger or whatever was available and attach it to a pail. Then we'd get some rope and lower it down for supplies, using the branch as a crude pulley. I'm not proud to admit it, but once in a great while we'd take the charity candy we were supposed to be selling and chuck it down on unsuspecting friends. Once we built a tree house in a maple behind a neighbor's house, but it was nothing more than a few planks hammered into the tree to make a platform. We never really got more elaborate than that, but my imagination supplied the rest, thanks in part to my favorite book, *The Swiss Family Robinson*.

We had a lot of sugar maples in our yard, and they were ideal climbing trees. For us there were two challenges: how high and how fast could we go. Sometimes we'd race. I loved climbing fast. You would think there was a tiger chasing me up the tree. I was fearless. We could spend hours in those trees, surveying the landscape, watching the sunset, calling out to each other, sometimes in made-up codes. It's hard to describe the feeling. It wasn't completely silent up there. You could hear birds tweeting, cars in the distance, a plane overhead, sometimes a door slamming or someone's mother yelling. But it was magical, and my imagination soared. I imagined what it was like for Orville and Wilbur Wright, two of my heroes, looking out from their cockpit on their first flight, or the first astronauts who saw our planet from outer space. Sometimes I'd pretend that I was the ruler over a vast land. Sometimes I was just happy to be myself, away from everyone trying to make me catch up in reading and talking.

I recently met a woman who has a farm with a walnut orchard where she hosts kids to "detox" or "withdraw" from electronics. She said the first two days are rough for the kids. They don't know what to do without their devices, and they seem lost and in a fog. But after a couple of days, the orchard becomes their playground. Some had never climbed a tree. They made up games and explored every feature of the woods and farm. I like this story because I really believe that while electronics are critical to many of our scientific advancements and the way we live now, the best and most important laboratory is the world we live in.

A CASTLE IN THE AIR

Once I learned to read, I'd often read the same book over and over. One of my favorites was *The Swiss Family Robinson* by Johann David Wyss, published in 1812. The author was a Swiss pastor who wrote the novel as a way of teaching his four sons to be resourceful, respectful, and brave. The story begins when the family is shipwrecked in the East Indies on their way from England to Australia. Each chapter brings a new challenge for the family as they learn to survive on the desert island. They were able to save some livestock from the ship; then they salvaged everything from the wreck including tools. As the family begins to explore the island, they discover all kinds of new plant and animal species. A monkey leads the way into a coconut grove that then provides the family with milk. Gourds are used for bowls and spoons.

In setting up the household, one of the sons observes that eagles build their nests in the trees to protect their young. Taking their inspiration from the eagle, the family embarks on constructing a magnificent tree house. They clear the rotten wood from inside the trunk of a tree, install the captain's door from the ship, and then build a spiral staircase with handrails from the base to the top, cutting in windows along the way for light and air. Eventually, they add running water by creating a reservoir that feeds the house through pipes and pours out into a turtle's shell.

To this day, I'll sometimes make up "what if" scenarios and then try to imagine how I would survive a shipwreck or a plane crash in the Arctic. I love those kinds of movies, too. Most recently, I liked Matt Damon in *The Martian*. His character, Watney, is a botanist who survives alone for four years on Mars after his crew leaves him behind. He figures out how to grow potatoes using the crew's poop to fertilize the Martian soil, and how to extract water from the leftover rocket fuel. The audience groaned when he used the poop, but he survived thanks to his knowledge of botany.

PROJECT #2
MODEL TREEHOUSE WITH PAPIER-MÂCHÉ TREE

You'll need:

- Newspaper
- Flour
- Water
- Mixing bowl
- Spoon (optional)
- Scissors
- Scotch tape
- Empty toilet paper roll,

Pringles can, or any round canister
- Cardboard
- Blow dryer (optional)
- Pipe cleaners or twigs
- Glue
- Paint
- Paintbrush

1 PAPIER-MÂCHÉ IS MESSY SO BE SURE TO START BY PUTTING DOWN SOME NEWSPAPER TO WORK ON.

3 CUT NEWSPAPER INTO STRIPS AN INCH WIDE AND 8-10 INCHES LONG.

2 PUT EQUAL PARTS FLOUR AND WATER IN A MIXING BOWL UNTIL THE CONSISTENCY IS LIKE PEA SOUP. IF THERE ARE LUMPS, SMOOTH THEM OUT BY STIRRING WITH A SPOON OR YOUR HANDS. TRIAL AND ERROR IS INVOLVED WITH GETTING THE CONSISTENCY OF THE FLOUR AND WATER RIGHT, SO ADD WATER SLOWLY. YOU CAN ALWAYS ADD MORE.

4 TAPE THE TUBE PERPENDICULAR TO THE CARDBOARD.

5 DIP THE STRIPS INTO THE MIXTURE, THEN RUN EACH STRIP BETWEEN YOUR FINGERS TO REMOVE EXCESS LIQUID.

6 APPLY THE STRIPS IN VERTICAL LAYERS FROM THE TOP OF THE TUBE TO THE CARDBOARD. THIS WILL CEMENT THE TUBE TO THE CARDBOARD. KEEP APPLYING STRIPS AROUND THE CYLINDER UNTIL THE BASE IS BUILT UP LIKE A TRUNK. LET THE TRUNK DRY. THIS WILL TAKE A DAY OR SO. (USE A BLOWDRYER FOR FASTER RESULTS.)

7 POKE HOLES IN THE TUBE WITH SCISSORS AND THEN BEND A PIPE CLEANER IN THE SHAPE OF A BRANCH AND INSERT IT INTO THE HOLE. CAREFULLY COVER IT WITH SMALLER NEWSPAPER STRIPS, OR JUST USE ACTUAL TWIGS.

8 ATTACH A STURDY PIECE OF CARDBOARD TO THE TOP OF THE TUBE EITHER WITH PAPIER-MÂCHÉ OR GLUE. THIS WILL BE THE PLATFORM FOR YOUR HOUSE.

9 PAINT YOUR TREE TRUNK.

NOTE: THIS IS WHERE YOU CAN BE REALLY CREATIVE AND IMPROVISE, MAKING FURNITURE OUT OF POPSICLE STICKS, PIPE CLEANERS, AND FABRIC. YOU CAN MAKE A ROPE LADDER OUT OF YARN AND TOOTHPICKS. RAID THE JUNK DRAWER, THE GARAGE, OR THE SEWING BASKET FOR ALL KINDS OF TREASURE YOU CAN TRANSFORM INTO HOUSEHOLD NECESSITIES, LIKE THE SWISS FAMILY ROBINSON DOES.

The maples in our backyard grew to be about 30 or 40 feet tall, though they can sometimes grow to over 100 feet. There are about 200 species of maple trees. The most common maples in New England where we lived are sugar, black, red, and silver. One of the coolest things about maples is the seed pods that fall from the trees in spring. They're officially called samaras, but we called them "keys." To many people they are better known as helicopters and whirligigs for the way they twirl when they fly. Samaras usually grow in pairs, with two "wings" and two seed pods in the middle. Because maple trees have extremely wide canopies, the seeds need to scatter farther out to find their own sunny place to grow. The wings help them do that. According to Amber Kanuckel in the 2019 *Farmers' Almanac*, the design is so ingenious that scientists have studied them for space exploration. Of course, my sister and I had no idea how those papery wings worked; we just loved to peel them open and stick them on our noses.

When you want to identify a tree, there are a few key components, namely the shape, leaves, bark, and root system. There are lots of trees you can probably identify just by sight, without consulting a field guide. Palm trees, for instance, are extremely tall with smooth bark that looks

We used to break these in half down the middle and stick them on our noses.

Wikimedia Commons/Feb981 at English Wikipedia

like an ACE bandage wrapped around a sprained wrist, a crown of fronds at the top, and no branches. Most conifers, which are a type of evergreen tree, are cone-shaped with needle-filled branches, perfect for hanging Christmas ornaments.

The two main tree groups are deciduous and evergreen. Deciduous trees lose their leaves every year in the fall and grow them back in the spring. Also known as broadleaf trees, they primarily grow in the eastern United States. I knew our maples were deciduous because their leaves fell off every autumn, and we raked them into huge piles and jumped into them for what seemed like hours. Most fruit trees are also deciduous. They produce flowers in the spring that have seeds, which in turn grow into fruit.

Evergreens, on the other hand, keep their foliage year-round. They usually have needles instead of broad leaves. These kinds of needled trees tend to produce pinecones, which carry and protect their seeds. Some examples of evergreens include hemlock, spruce, and white fir. If you live in Florida, California, or a tropical area, you're probably familiar with palm trees. They belong to yet another category of trees called Arecaceae and have more in common with shrubs, except they can grow to 197 feet. The reason they are so skinny is because without a lot of water, they don't have the capacity to grow wide trunks. And the trees, searching for sunlight, grow taller and taller. At the top, their leaves are arranged like fans. And they bear fruit: coconuts.

PROJECT # 3
PINECONE ANIMALS

The great thing about a pinecone is that its shape can look like the body of almost any animal. On its side, you can make a moose or a dog; if you flip it the other way, you can make an owl or a penguin. Here are instructions for an owl.

You'll need:

- Paint and paintbrush or spray paint (optional)
- Pinecones (If you don't have them where you live, you can find them at a crafts store.)
- Scissors
- Felt of various colors
- Glue
- Buttons
- Pipe cleaners or dried kidney beans (optional)
- Bottle cap (optional)

INSTRUCTIONS

1. PAINT (OR SPRAY-PAINT) YOUR PINECONE OR LEAVE IT NATURAL.

2. TO MAKE THE EYES, CUT A PIECE OF FELT INTO A WIDE HEART. THIS WILL BE THE OWL'S MASK. CUT OUT FELT CIRCLES AND GLUE THEM TO THE FELT HEART WHERE THE EYES WOULD BE. ADD BUTTONS FOR PUPILS.

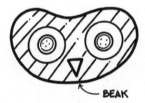

BEAK

3. CUT OUT A YELLOW OR ORANGE TRIANGLE FOR YOUR BEAK AND GLUE IT TO THE MASK.

4. FOR WINGS, CUT OUT TWO IDENTICAL-SIZED PIECES OF FELT SHAPED LIKE TEARDROPS AND GLUE THEM ONTO THE SIDES OF YOUR PINECONE WITH THE POINTY ENDS OF THE TEARDROPS FACING DOWN.

5. TO MAKE TALONS, IMPROVISE WITH KIDNEY BEANS, PIPE CLEANERS, OR FELT.

6. TO KEEP YOUR OWL FROM TIPPING OVER, SET IT ON AN UPSIDE-DOWN, FLAT BOTTLE CAP OR MAKE A RING OUT OF PIPE CLEANERS.

In order to identify a tree correctly, you need to examine the leaves. Leaves, as you probably know, are responsible for keeping the tree alive, which is remarkable given how soft and delicate leaves are compared to the mammoth size of trees. But through the process of photosynthesis, leaves, or more accurately the pigment chlorophyll, absorb energy from the sun and transform it into sugar that the tree uses for food. Chlorophyll is also the stuff in leaves that gives them their green color. It's the combination of energy from the sun, water from the soil, and carbon dioxide from the air that produces sugars, also called glucose. During photosynthesis, special structures in plant cells called chloroplasts separate water into hydrogen and oxygen, and the oxygen gets released back into the atmosphere through the small pores on leaves. This is the air that we breathe.

Chlorophyll, or the lack of chlorophyll, is also responsible for leaves changing color in the fall. When the shorter and colder days in fall and winter come around, there is less sunlight for plants to absorb. The green pigment in chlorophyll breaks down, allowing other pigments to come through. This is the time of fall when you will see brilliant reds, oranges, and yellows. As the chlorophyll fades, the base of the stem of a leaf softens until the leaf finally falls off. The tree responds by sealing the gap, similar to how our blood clots to stop a wound from bleeding. Fallen leaves even form leaf scars.

THE LEAF WHISPERER

Andy Goldsworthy was thrilled when he was accepted to art school, until he got there. He found he didn't like working in the cramped studio spaces. He took off for the beach one day and found he loved being outside, observing nature. "I learnt so much in that couple of hours. And I shifted to working outside. I didn't really go back in again." You will be blown away if you search Google Images for Andy Goldsworthy's art. He primarily uses stone, wood, leaves, and ice. He is known as a "land artist," and much of what he constructs goes back to nature the way sandcastles go back to the sea. In the fall, he creates circles or wreaths out of the fallen leaves, using their vibrant colors in circular patterns. Some of his projects are ice sculptures, stone walls, or enormous stone sculptures that take a team of craftspeople to assemble. What they all have in common, besides using material from nature, is that they require repetitive, methodical work.

Goldsworthy connects his love for this kind of work to his childhood, when he worked on farms in northern England. Most of the boys wanted to drive the tractors, but he liked the manual labor and being exposed to nature. "We often forget that we are nature. Nature is not something separate from us. So, when we say that we have lost our connection to nature, we've lost our connection to ourselves." By using art to commune with nature, Goldsworthy helps keep that connection alive.

PROJECT #4
PATTERNS FOUND IN NATURE

Goldsworthy's art projects are made in nature and don't use any man-made materials like glue or nails to hold them together. Try not to cheat! Find a spot in your yard or a local park to create your design.

You'll need:
- Leaves, twigs, or rocks
- Camera

INSTRUCTIONS

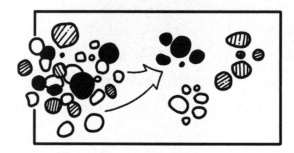

1. COLLECT A LOT OF LEAVES (OR TWIGS OR ROCKS) AND SORT THEM BY COLOR AND SIZE.

2. ARRANGE YOUR LEAVES INTO A PATTERN. GOLDSWORTHY ARRANGES LEAVES IN A RING FROM THE LIGHTEST COLOR AT THE CENTER OF THE CIRCLE TO THE DARKEST ON THE OUTTER RING. SIMILARLY, HE STARTS WITH SMALL ROCKS OR TWIGS AND BUILDS OUT TO THE LARGEST. YOU CAN ARRANGE THEM HOWEVER YOU'D LIKE.

3. WHEN YOU'RE FINISHED, TAKE A PICTURE. THEN TAKE A PICTURE OF YOUR CREATION AS OFTEN AS POSSIBLE (ONCE A DAY OR SO, IF YOU CAN) AND DOCUMENT THE WAY WIND AND WEATHER, HUMANS AND ANIMALS MIGHT CHANGE THINGS UP. GOLDSWORTHY DOCUMENTED ALL HIS PROJECTS.

There are four main things to look for when you're identifying leaves:

- Shape
- Veins
- Edges
- Arrangement on the stem

The shape can be like a hand, a spear, or a heart; it can be round or oval, flat or spindly. Even though we don't think of them as leaves, the needles on a pine tree, spikes on a cactus, and petals on the end of an asparagus stalk are all different kinds of leaves. The veins on some leaves grow from the base of the leaf to the edge on a diagonal. Others are like the veins in your body that go from big to small and then into thread-like capillaries near the edges of the leaves. The edges of leaves are another important feature. Are they smooth or jagged like a saw? Finally, the way leaves are arranged on the stem can differ widely. There are three basic patterns: opposite, which means that leaves grow on the same place on the left and right sides of the stem; alternate, which means they "take turns" climbing up the stem like footprints; or whorled, which is when they swirl around the stem, like an artichoke's leaves. Sunflowers are known for the fascinating arrangement of their seeds, which follow the mathematical pattern known as the Fibonacci sequence.

The sunflower is a beautiful example of a mathematical pattern found in nature.

JEANNE/JEAN

In 1740s France, women were not allowed to go to school, and peasant women like Jeanne Baret had no access to education. But as a child, Jeanne developed a love of plants and acquired a wide body of information about their medicinal benefits, much of it passed down for generations. She became what was called an "herb woman." Botany was a new science, and collecting plants wasn't regarded as a serious endeavor. Still, everyone from pharmacists to midwives relied on herb women to supply herbal remedies.

Baret worked as a housekeeper for a man named Philibert Commerson, who was chosen to collect plants as chief naturalist on a French expedition to the Americas. The expedition was in search of new lands to supply France with timber, medicine, and spices. Baret asked Commerson to take her with him. He agreed, but there was only one problem: it was against French law for women to travel by ship. Desperate to make the journey, Baret disguised herself as a man on a ship of 330 men. She changed her name from Jeanne to Jean, dressed as a young man, and worked hard to fit in and not draw attention to herself.

In addition to collecting over 500 species of plants, Baret became the first woman to travel around the world. But because of her status as a woman, she did not receive the praise or honors reserved for men. Commerson would have over 70 species named after him; Jeanne only one: the bareti (a now extinct species of sea snail). Baret's biographer, Glynis Ridley, speculates that for Baret it was all worth it just to witness the magnificence of the high seas—the flying fish, the manta rays, the sea turtles. The French Ministry of the Navy did eventually grant her a pension in recognition of her achievements expanding French knowledge of the plants of the world.

When I was younger, I had a lot of fun keeping a field guide to trees and leaves, recording all the information I could gather. I didn't wear a lab coat, but I often imagined myself in a laboratory. When I got a microscope for Christmas, I put almost anything small enough to fit under the lens to get a closer look. In order to check my leaf identification, I consulted our set of *Encyclopedia Britannica*, which was basically Google before Google existed. Though the encyclopedia stopped publishing print editions in 2012, you can now find it online. It's a great resource for tree identification. Whether using a book or online information, it's exciting to gather a bunch of leaves and get to work identifying them, sorting them by shape, edges, veins, and arrangement.

I never paid much attention to bark as a kid, but I've since learned that it has many layers, and it's as important to the tree as skin is to us. The outer layer protects the tree from the elements: sun, wind, and snow, as well as bacteria and molds. But bark is also part of the ecosystem. An ecosystem is the way all living organisms, including plants and animals, and the environment work together. Bark provides food and shelter for certain birds, animals, insects, and moss. Once you start looking at the bark on various trees, you'll see a tremendous variety of appearances and textures: sandpaper-like, veiny, notched, flaky, smooth, papery to the touch. The bark is the newest part of the tree, and just beneath it is the cambium.

You've probably learned that you can figure out the age of a tree by counting its rings, but for each ring that you count to determine age, you're counting two rings. One entire year is represented by a lighter band of cambium and a thinner, darker band of cambium measured together. The light-colored band shows growth during the warmer, rainier months and good growth conditions. And the dark-colored band shows growth during the colder months. A thinner band can also indicate less growth and worse conditions, such as drought, fire, or unusual temperatures. Trees grow outward, meaning that the center of a tree is the oldest part, and the outer rings the newest.

Beneath the cambium is inner bark, or phloem. The phloem delivers the food made during photosynthesis from the leaves to the rest of the tree. The central core, or heartwood, is the strongest wood in the tree even though it's no longer alive. It's protected from air and other elements and gives the tree its strength. Because human records of daily weather conditions only go back a century and a half, trees serve as useful tools for scientists studying climate change. Trees often live hundreds of years and can tell us about weather conditions long before humans started keeping track.

THE FATHER OF DENDROCHRONOLOGY (of what?)

Andrew Ellicott Douglass spent nearly two decades collecting tree samples from archeological sites, such as Pueblo Bonito and Aztec Ruins in New Mexico. In using tree rings to learn about historical climates, he gave rise to a branch of science known as dendro-chronology, which concerns itself with dating tree rings and studying the information we can learn about the environment from doing so. His work would ultimately reveal a 2,000-year record of climate conditions. Today, Douglass's legacy can be seen in the dozen large labs and 4,000 sites globally where data is being gathered and made available in the Tree Ring Database. I like the way dendrochronologist Valerie Trouet puts it: "Trees remember. They record history and they don't lie." They record rainfall, droughts, disease, fire, insect infestation, volcanic activity, and glaciers, all inside the rings of trees. And by telling us about how human activity impacts the environment over decades, these stories can help us with the critical job of understanding the future of climate change.

Arizona State Museum, University of Arizona, Charles Herbert, Photographer

Douglass in front of a cross section of a giant sequoia tree trunk (twice his size). You can see the markers that indicate different historical periods.

MEASURE A TREE

You'll need:
- Cloth tape measure
- Tree
- Calculator
- Google or a guide to trees

More information on tree growth can be found in "How Old Is My Tree?" by Lindsay Purcell, which you can find at purduelandscapereport.org.

INSTRUCTIONS

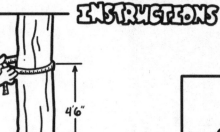

1. MEASURE THE CIRCUMFERENCE OF (DISTANCE AROUND) YOUR TREE AT APPROXIMATELY 4.5 FEET FROM THE GROUND WITH YOUR CLOTH TAPE MEASURE.

$$20 \div 3.14 = 6.36$$
CIRCUMFERENCE OF YOUR TREE — PI

2. USE YOUR CALCULATOR TO DIVIDE THAT NUMBER BY PI (3.14).

$$6.369 \times 3 = \text{GROWTH FACTOR}$$

3. MULTIPLY THAT NUMBER BY THE "GROWTH FACTOR" OF YOUR TREE. THE "GROWTH FACTOR" IS AN AVERAGE ESTIMATE OF YOUR TREES GROWTH OVER TIME. THE INTERNATIONAL SOCIETY OF ARBORICULTURE HAS PUBLISHED A TABLE OF GROWTH FACTOR NUMBERS ACCORDING TO TREE SPECIES THAT YOU NEED TO GOOGLE OR LOOK UP IN A GUIDE TO TREES TO COMPLETE THE FORMULA FOR MEASURING YOUR TREE.

19.108

I'M 19! TIME TO GO SEE THE WORLD!

4. THE RESULT IS THE AGE OF YOUR TREE. FOR EXAMPLE: IF MY SILVER MAPLE IS 20 INCHES IN CIRCUMFERENCE, AND I DIVIDE THAT BY 3.14, I GET 6.369. I MULTIPLY THAT BY THE GROWTH FACTOR (3) AND GET 19.108. MY TREE IS APPROXIMATELY 19 YEARS OLD.

PROJECT #6
FIELD GUIDE TO TREES

You'll need:

- Tree to identify
- Pencil
- Notebook or sketchbook
- Crayon (optional)
- Access to the internet or an encyclopedia

INSTRUCTIONS

1.

FIND A TREE YOU WANT TO IDENTIFY, WHETHER FROM YOUR LOCAL PARK, A WOODED WALKING TRAIL, OR YOUR OWN BACKYARD.

SHAPE - WIDER THAN TALL - THICK TRUNK

2. ONCE YOU'VE FOUND YOUR TREE, YOU'LL WANT TO NOTE ITS MOST DISTINCTIVE FEATURES. USE YOUR PENCIL TO DRAW ITS BASIC SHAPE IN YOUR NOTEBOOK. NOTE THE TREE'S LEAVES. YOU CAN EITHER DRAW WHAT ITS LEAVES LOOK LIKE WITH A PENCIL OR MAKE AN IMPRESSION OF A LEAF. IF YOU WANT TO MAKE A LEAF IMPRESSION, PLACE THE LEAF IN YOUR NOTEBOOK UNDERNEATH THE PAGE. TAKE A CRAYON WITH ITS PAPER COVERING REMOVED AND USE ITS LONG SIDE TO RUB THE PAPER OVER THE LEAF. AN IMPRESSION OF THE LEAF SHOULD COME THROUGH.

HOW DO THE LEAVES GROW? OPPOSITE OR ALTERNATE?

WHAT DO THE VEINS LOOK LIKE?

NUTS OR SEEDS?

BE SURE TO NOTE CERTAIN CHARACTERISTICS:
HOW DO THE LEAVES GROW ON THE BRANCH? DO THEY GROW OPPOSITE EACH OTHER? DO THEY ALTERNATE? WHAT DO THE VEINS LOOK LIKE? ARE THERE ANY FRUITS OR SEEDS OR CONES GROWING ON THE BRANCHES? WHAT DO THEY LOOK LIKE?

BARK SAMPLE

3. SKETCH WHAT THE BARK LOOKS LIKE. IF POSSIBLE, TAKE A SMALL SAMPLE AND MAKE A CRAYON IMPRESSION.

(CONTINUED)

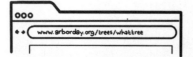

www.arborday.org/trees/whattree

④ ONCE YOU'VE COLLECTED ENOUGH INFORMATION, RETURN HOME AND USE THE INFORMATION YOU RECORDED IN YOUR NOTEBOOK TO FIND OUT WHAT TREE YOU WERE LOOKING AT. YOU CAN DO THIS BY CHECKING THE ARBOR DAY FOUNDATION'S "WHAT TREE IS THAT?: TREE IDENTIFICATION FIELD GUIDE" ON THE ARBORDAY.ORG WEBSITE OR BY GOING TO YOUR LOCAL LIBRARY FOR A FIELD GUIDE TO TREES. ONE I LIKE IS PUBLISHED BY THE BROOKLYN BOTANIC GARDEN: *THE TREE BOOK FOR KIDS* AND *THEIR GROWN-UPS*.

⑤

CHECK BACK WITH YOUR TREE EVERY MONTH AND SEE IF THERE ARE ANY CHANGES. IF IT'S FLOWERING IT IS READY TO PRODUCE FRUIT. IS THERE SAP? GENERALLY, YOU SHOULD SEE SAP IN THE SPRING. YOU MAY SEE SOME DURING THE REST OF THE YEAR BECAUSE YOUR TREE HAS BEEN HURT OR DISEASED. HAVE THE LEAVES CHANGED COLOR OR DROPPED? IF SO, IT'S FALL AND WITH LESS SUNLIGHT THE LEAVES LOSE THEIR GREEN; TURN RED, ORANGE, AND YELLOW; BECOME BRITTLE; AND FALL.

When I was around six, I was obsessed with rhododendrons, probably because we had huge bushes of them all around our house. They were eye level, so I was able to watch them bloom every spring as if in slow motion.

Every day, I would observe the various stages of development. One thing I noticed was that the blossoms didn't all bloom at the same time. On different parts of the bush, some were barely peeping, meaning they were tightly closed like a fist, while others were beginning to open, and others had completely bloomed. I've always had a scientific mind, which means I loved

The rhododendron bud.

Wikimedia Commons/Vulkano Uwe Horst Friese, Bremerhaven

Wikimedia Commons/Randy Smith

Partially opened . . .

Fully opened. You can see down the flower's speckled "throat."

observing, categorizing, and understanding how things worked. I used to take the buds apart and examine the different stages of development. On this page and the page opposite are photos that show three stages of development.

If you cut a bud in half, you can see all the parts of the flower. From outside to inside: the petals (which protect the seed and then, when they blossom, attract insects with their bright colors), the anther (which produces pollen), the stigma (where the pollen rests), the ovary (the part that protects the egg cell), and the receptacle (the thick part of the stem where the flower grows out).

PROJECT #7
PRESSING FLOWERS

You'll need:

- Flowers
- Wax paper
- 3 heavy books
- Frame, envelope, spray paint, glue, note cards (optional)

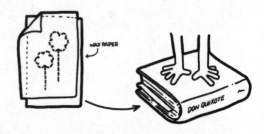
WAX PAPER

DON QUIXOTE

1. PICK SOME FLOWERS FROM OUTSIDE.
EXPERIMENT WITH TINY FLOWERS, LIKE
BUTTERCUPS, AND LARGER ONES, LIKE ROSES.
REALLY BIG FLOWERS, LIKE PEONIES, WILL
PROBABLY BE TOO DIFFICULT TO PRESS, BUT
YOU CAN USE SOME OF THEIR PETALS AND
ARRANGE THEM. (BE SURE YOU'RE PICKING
FLOWERS YOU'RE ALLOWED TO PICK AND NOT
USING SOMEONE'S PRIZED GARDEN FOR
THIS PROJECT!)

2. ARRANGE THE PETALS OR PRESS THE FLOWERS
BETWEEN TWO PIECES OF WAX PAPER, THEN PUT
THEM INSIDE AN OVERSIZED BOOK AND APPLY AS
MUCH WEIGHT TO THE BOOK AS POSSIBLE BY PUTTING
OTHER HEAVY BOOKS ON TOP OF IT. YOU CAN CHECK
IT EVERY DAY, BUT IT'S BEST TO LET IT STAY PRESSED
FOR ABOUT A WEEK BEFORE TAKING YOUR PRESSED
FLOWERS OUT.

3. NOW YOU CAN TRANSFER THE FLOWER TO A FRAME, PUT SOME
PETALS IN A LETTER, SPRAY-PAINT THEM AND MAKE A COLLAGE,
OR GLUE THEM TO NOTE CARDS. THESE ARE JUST A FEW IDEAS.
BE CREATIVE! YOU CAN DO A LOT WITH YOUR PRESSED FLOWERS.

Every year when I was in elementary school, we visited an apple orchard to pick apples in the fall. We mostly picked McIntosh apples, which are popular in the Northeast. Even though we say things like "American as apple pie," apples originally came from Central Asia and were brought to America by European colonists. Apples grow best with plenty of sun and space, which is why orchards are spread out in long rows. There are between 7,500 and 10,000 different cultivated varieties of apples, and that doesn't take into account wild apples. The variety of apples is a result of cross-pollination among species over hundreds of years. If you've ever had a wild apple, you've probably noticed that it's pretty small and bitter. You wouldn't want to eat it. The apples we enjoy today have been cultivated by farmers and vary in size, color, shape, and taste. The skin can vary in thickness and the flesh in sweetness and texture. The skin protects the pulp and flesh of the apple, and the stem holds the core together and connects the fruit to the tree.

In the spring, most apple trees produce pink or white blossoms with five petals. These are pollinated by honeybees that deliver pollen from the male part of the flower (anther) to the female part of the flower (stigma). The next time you eat an apple, turn it upside down and you'll see the remnant of the flower, also known as the eye of the apple.

AN APPLE A DAY KEEPS THE DOCTOR AWAY

They say he wore clothes made from burlap sacks, often went without shoes, and wore a tin pot for a hat that doubled for making apple cider. Johnny Appleseed was born in 1774 and came from my home state, Massachusetts. His real name was John Chapman and he was a frontier nurseryman, meaning he left the East Coast for the western frontier, where he helped to plant orchards. His father was a farmer, and Chapman learned about growing crops from an early age, eventually taking his expertise to Pennsylvania, Ohio, Indiana, and Illinois. From pictures, I always had the idea that he walked across the country and threw seeds wherever he went. In truth, he planted orderly orchards, cared for them, and eventually owned 1,200 acres. You probably wouldn't want to eat Chapman's apples. They were small, hard, and bitter and mostly used for making applejack, which is not a breakfast cereal. It's hard cider, which means it has alcohol content.

Chapman didn't just love apples. His love of nature was so great that, according to Michael Pollan's book *The Botany of Desire*, he was said to put out a campfire rather than let a mosquito get burned by the flame. He bought lame horses to keep them from being put down. He once saved a wolf from a trap, nursed him back to health, and then kept him as a pet. One night he found a hollowed-out log to sleep in, only to discover bear cubs curled up inside. According to Pollan, he let them stay while he slept in the snow. He looked at the world from the point of view of plants and animals. We have that in common. I wish more people would.

PROJECT #8
PLANTING AN APPLE TREE

You'll need:
- Kitchen knife
- 3–4 apples
- Paper towels
- Plastic bag with an airtight seal
- Marker
- Fridge
- Pot and soil to fill it, or an outdoor patch of ground
- Water

NOTE: THIS IS A LONG-TERM PROJECT. IT COULD TAKE THREE YEARS FOR YOUR APPLE TREE TO START MAKING APPLES.

1. USE YOUR KITCHEN KNIFE TO CUT YOUR APPLES IN HALF AND CAREFULLY REMOVE THE SEEDS. (MAKE SURE TO ASK A GROWN-UP FOR PERMISSION BEFORE YOU USE A SHARP KNIFE.) THE MORE SEEDS YOU HAVE THE HIGHER THE CHANCES ONE OF THEM WILL GROW INTO A TREE, SO GET SEEDS FROM A FEW APPLES TO INCREASE YOUR ODDS.

2. LET THE SEEDS DRY IN A WARM PLACE FOR THREE DAYS.

3. PLACE YOUR SEEDS IN A DAMP PAPER TOWEL AND PUT THEM IN A PLASTIC BAG, THEN SEAL THE BAG. DATE THE BAG WITH YOUR MARKER AND PLACE IT IN THE FRIDGE. THE FRIDGE WILL FOOL THE SEEDS INTO THINKING IT'S WINTER, WHICH THEY NEED TO GROW. YOUR SEEDS WILL TAKE BETWEEN A FEW WEEKS AND A FEW MONTHS TO BEGIN GROWING SHOOTS.

4. CHECK YOUR SEEDS EVERY WEEK TO MAKE SURE THE PAPER TOWEL IS STILL DAMP. ONCE YOU SEE A LITTLE PROTRUSION THAT LOOKS LIKE A WORM COMING OUT OF YOUR SEED, IT'S TIME TO PLANT.

HOLY COW! IT WORKED!

6.

5. TRANSFER YOUR SEEDS FROM THE PLASTIC BAG TO A POT FILLED WITH SOIL. PLANT THEM SO THAT THE SPROUT IS ABOVE THE SOIL. YOU CAN ALSO PLANT YOUR SEEDS OUTSIDE IF YOU HAVE THE SPACE; YOU JUST NEED TO MAKE SURE YOU PLANT THEM DURING THE SPRING IN A SUNNY SPOT. REMEMBER TO WATER YOUR TREE WHEN THE SOIL IS DRY!

IN A FEW YEARS, YOUR APPLE TREE SHOULD START BEARING APPLES. THEY WON'T TASTE OR LOOK LIKE THE APPLES YOU GOT THE SEEDS FROM. THEY WILL BE MORE LIKE JOHNNY APPLESEED'S BECAUSE MOST APPLE TREES CAN'T SELF-POLLINATE. THEY NEED INSECTS, WIND, OR PEOPLE TO CARRY POLLEN FROM ONE TREE TO ANOTHER. THIS MEANS THE APPLE YOU ARE TRYING TO GROW MAY CONTAIN SEEDS FROM A DIFFERENT KIND OF APPLE ALTOGETHER.

Once, when I was eating an apple, I accidentally swallowed some of the seeds. My sister said a tree was going to grow inside my stomach. That freaked me out just a little bit, but then my brother said the seeds were poisonous and totally freaked me out. When I consulted our encyclopedia, I discovered that the seeds have something called amygdalin in them, which is a cyanide-based molecule. I knew that cyanide was poison. My brother was right! I was in big trouble. Fortunately, I kept reading and discovered that the cyanide from an apple seed is only harmful if *crushed*. That and the fact that you'd need to ingest at least 150 seeds, if not thousands, to do any damage. I wanted to figure out how many apples I would need to eat to consume 150 seeds (just in case). Every apple has five seed compartments, which are called carpels. Each carpel has at least one seed and sometimes two (on occasion up to thirteen seeds per apple). That would be 30 apples. So, if you accidentally swallow some seeds while you're eating an apple, you have absolutely nothing to worry about. If you have a big brother or sister, you should still be careful. If they are anything like mine, they will stop at nothing to freak you out.

PROJECT # 9
CITIZEN SCIENCE PROJECTS ON PLANTS AND TREES

Kids can become involved in collecting data for real scientific projects. Some of these things that can be monitored are numbers of different types of plants in your community. The data can be compiled to determine if a certain species is either increasing or decreasing. You can find more information about this online. If you'd like to become part of the data collection community, National Geographic has an extensive list of projects available at nationalgeographic.org/idea/citizen-science-projects. You can also become a plant monitor through the National Phenology Network's Nature's Notebook. Visit usanpn.org/partner to find out more.

BIRDS

CHAPTER FOUR

I f you asked me what my top wish was as a kid, I would have told you that I wanted to fly. My first actual flight was in a Lockheed Electra airplane, and I was twelve years old. It was also my first experience with changing air pressure, which was horrible. Many autistic people have extreme sensitivity to pressure, and the pain was torture. But once we got to cruising altitude, I was fine, mesmerized by the clouds below us. They looked like white hills you could walk on. Another memory of flight was watching seagulls on Martha's Vineyard. They could soar without moving their wings by catching the wind's currents—like a glider. I loved kites. We made simple ones with sticks and paper, but I also had a fancy kite with the wings angled backward. I could fly it on the beach for what seemed like hours, watching it sail and turn in the air currents. I used to fly a lot in my dreams, gliding through the air or moving my arms like the breaststroke.

PROJECT #1
BASIC KITE

You'll need:

- Handsaw
- 2 ¼ " dowels (One dowel should be 24 inches long and the other should be 20 inches long.)
- Twine
- Electrical tape

- 1 large sheet of newspaper, a plastic bag, or wrapping paper
- Scissors
- String
- Ribbon

Tip: The cross arm may need to be bowed to make the kite fly better. Bend the cross arm slightly by tensioning a string on the back of the kite between the ends of the cross arm.

INSTRUCTIONS

1. USE YOUR HANDSAW (WITH GROWN-UP SUPERVISION) TO NOTCH THE ENDS OF THE DOWELS, WHICH MAKES AN INDENTATION OR SLOT TO RUN THE TWINE THROUGH.

2. CROSS THE DOWELS IN A T SHAPE AND BIND THEM TOGETHER WITH TWINE SO THAT THEY ARE FIRMLY CONNECTED. THEN RUN ELECTRICAL TAPE OVER THE TWINE FOR EXTRA STRENGTH.

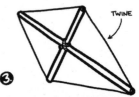

3. RUN THE TWINE THROUGH THE NOTCHES YOU MADE AT THE ENDS OF YOUR DOWELS. THIS IS THE FRAME OF YOUR KITE.

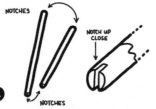

4. SET THE FRAME DOWN ON NEWSPAPER OR A PLASTIC BAG. FOR A FANCY KITE, USE WRAPPING PAPER.

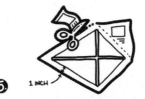

5. USE YOUR SCISSORS TO CUT THE PAPER ALL AROUND THE FRAME LEAVING AN EXTRA INCH OF PAPER STICKING OUT PAST THE FRAME.

6. FOLD THE EXTRA INCH TOWARD THE INSIDE OF THE FRAME AND TAPE IT DOWN.

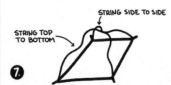

7. RUN A LENGTH OF STRING FROM THE TOP TO THE BOTTOM AND ANOTHER LENGTH OF STRING ACROSS THE T.

8. WHERE THESE TWO STRINGS CROSS IS THE SPOT TO TIE YOUR FLYING STRING.

9. AT THE BOTTOM OF THE KITE, ATTACH ONE MORE PIECE OF TWINE ABOUT TWO FEET LONG, AND EVERY FEW INCHES, TIE A PIECE OF RIBBON. THIS IS THE TAIL. YOU'RE READY TO GO!

As an engineer, I'm really impressed with how birds fly. Everything about them is tailored to make flight possible. First, of course, are feathers. They are strong, light, flexible, and key to keeping birds warm. They also act as camouflage from predators. Small birds may replace their feathers one to three times per year in a process called "molting," sort of like a snake shedding its skin. Very large birds may have partial molts and replace only part of their feathers. The shape of a bird's wings is also instrumental. They're curved in a way that allows them to produce enough force to give birds lift. Birds have developed powerful muscles so they can flap their wings hard enough to fly.

I loved to watch birds soar. I still do.

And the rest of many birds' bodies are also geared toward making flight easier. They have extremely lightweight beaks and mostly hollow bones. Ever wonder how some birds can land on a surface as thin as a branch or telephone wire? The answer is their powerful eyesight. And their landing gear, their talons, are also incredibly strong and lightweight.

People have always wanted to fly and have been telling stories about doing so since ancient Greece. As the Greek myth goes, Icarus's father, Daedalus, made two pairs of wings from feathers and wax so he and his son could escape the tower where they were imprisoned. Daedalus warned his son not to fly too close to the sun, but Icarus didn't heed his father's advice and soared higher and higher until the sun melted the wax, causing him to fall into the sea. People use the expression "Don't fly too close to the sun," meaning be careful, don't be too ambitious, don't fly too high.

But it took a great deal of ambition, ingenuity, and perseverance for humans to achieve liftoff. Before there were planes, people invented hot air balloons and dirigibles, or what we think of as blimps, to get into the skies. Neither proved very effective for flying. They were easily affected by weather conditions and difficult to maneuver. Early aviation attempts made the mistake of attempting to copy birds. People thought if they could make wings that flapped, they could fly. The problem was humans would need a massive wingspan in proportion to their bodies, almost 22 feet. And a wingspan that size would be too heavy to get off the ground. It's also important to remember that birds are incredibly strong relative to their size. It was only when propellers were discovered to be much more effective at moving air under wings than flapping that humans touched the skies. Even though it was impossible

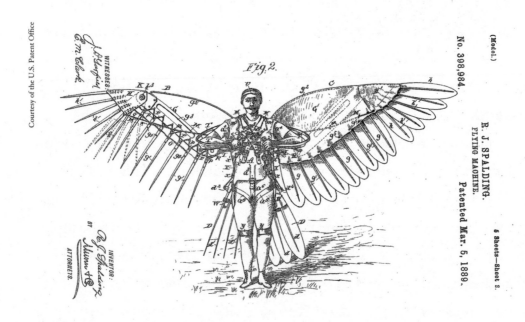

Would you want to fly in this 1889 U.S. patented "Flying Machine"?

to fly like a bird, the U.S. Patent and Trademark Office issued patent 398984 for a flying machine to R. J. Spalding.

The Wright brothers, who are two of my heroes, were the first inventors to make a successful airplane. They received their first patent in 1903 for the "Flying Machine" after decades of trial and error. They started with gliders, then added lightweight gasoline engines and propellers. They tested and adjusted their planes nearly 1,000 times before successfully controlling the plane, which involved mastering pitch, roll, and yaw (moving the plane up and down, left and right, and tilting side to side). Of course, birds do all this by instinct, and for as long as people have marveled at their ability to soar through the air, we have been trying to soar alongside them.

Even though flapping was the wrong idea to get planes off the ground, aircraft do borrow some ideas from birds. Plane wings have flaps that can move up or down to speed the plane up for takeoff or slow it down for landing, much like how birds angle their wings to control their flight. If you've ever looked closely at a plane, you'll notice that it has a rear rudder, which is the part of the plane at the tail end and looks like a vertical triangle with a flat top. It serves the same purpose as a bird's tail: controlling direction by directing the air flow. Watch birds when they land. You can often see them moving their tails back and forth to steer. You might also have noticed that plane wings tip up at their ends. These tips are called winglets and were first developed by NASA to reduce drag, which is airflow that slows a plane. Observing the tilted-up ends of raptors' wings, engineers began designing planes with tipped ends and found they reduced drag by 20 percent, which also saved fuel.

PROJECT # 2
BASIC GLIDER

Take these simple steps and experiment with different materials, like balsa wood or Styrofoam. You might try making landing gear or planes of different sizes.

You'll need:

- Scissors
- 2 cardboard egg cartons (with flat tops)
- Precision blade
- Marker
- Scotch tape
- Penny or nickel

INSTRUCTIONS

1. FIRST, USE YOUR SCISSORS TO CUT OFF THE BOTTOMS OF THE EGG CARTONS. YOU'LL ONLY NEED THE TOPS.

2. NEXT, USE YOUR MARKER TO DRAW THE OUTLINE OF YOUR GLIDER ON THE TOPS OF THE EGG CARTONS, THEN CUT OUT THE PIECES. THERE ARE THREE PIECES YOU'LL NEED TO CUT OUT:
- BODY
- HORIZONTAL STABILIZER
- WINGS

3. TO ASSEMBLE YOUR GLIDER, MAKE A SLIT IN THE SIDE OF THE GLIDER'S BODY THAT'S BIG ENOUGH TO SLIP THE WINGS INTO.

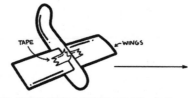

TO KEEP THE WINGS LEVEL AND SECURE THEM FROM WOBBLING, TAPE THEM IN PLACE.

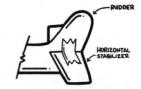

CUT ANOTHER SLIT RIGHT UNDER THE RUDDER TO SLIP THE HORIZONTAL STABILIZER INTO, AND TAPE THAT IN PLACE AS WELL.

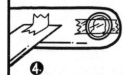

4. TO STABILIZE YOUR GLIDER, YOU'LL NEED TO ADD SOME WEIGHT TO THE FRONT. TAPE A COIN (A PENNY OR NICKEL WORKS BEST) ONTO THE NOSE OF YOUR GLIDER.

5. YOUR GLIDER IS NOW READY FOR FLIGHT. IF IT DOESN'T PERFORM AT FIRST, MAKE MODIFICATIONS: MORE WEIGHT, LESS WEIGHT, DIFFERENT SIZE WINGS, ETC. EXPERIMENT.

For a long time, people didn't think birds were very smart. When I was growing up, kids used the term "bird brain" to tease each other because it meant "stupid." I had to deal with a fair amount of teasing because of my difference. I couldn't figure out why I didn't fit in, so I focused my energies on the things I loved to do, like riding and taking care of horses, which is how I came to spend a lot of time in barns. It was there I first encountered the small blue birds known as barn swallows that make their homes there.

The swallows weren't afraid of me or the horses. They flew in and out of the barn while I groomed and fed the horses and cleaned out the stalls. I'd watch the swallows nose-dive and circle back to their nests under the eaves and marvel at their speed and fearlessness.

I thought that the birds must have grown accustomed to humans, and that might have been true, but there was another reason they stuck around nearby: our presence has a value for the birds, because we tend to shake up the insect world, which creates perfect feeding grounds for barn swallows. They are what's known as "insectivores," meaning they mostly eat insects. They catch flies while in flight and drink by skimming over rivers or ponds, scooping up water—and sometimes insects along with it—with their open beaks.

Wherever they live, barn swallows build their cup-shaped nests out of mud clots and line them with grasses and feathers, which provide a soft bedding. If you're in a barn or other man-made structure that's tall and has beams, like an airplane

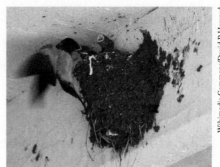

I first saw barn swallows like these in the barn where I groomed the horses.

Wikimedia Commons/David P Howard

hangar, it's likely that swallows have made it their home. Scan the beams for nests; often there are multiple nests on a given beam. Before barns and hangars were around, swallows used to live in caves. Barn swallows are now the largest population in the swallow family, which tells you something very important: they are good at adapting. Birds have even learned how to use automatic doors to gain access to their nests located inside parking garages or in lumberyards.

SURVIVAL OF THE FITTEST

Charles Darwin was a naturalist in the making from the time he could walk. Whether at home, boarding school, or college, he collected whatever he could find in the natural world: butterflies, pebbles, shells, stones, oysters, bugs, plants, mice, and—his favorite—beetles. He categorized them and observed differences in the species and kept notes. Why do specimens of the same species of bird have different beaks? Why does one kind of beetle have a shiny back and another dull? According to one story, Darwin was once so excited about finding three unusual beetles that he put one in his mouth to carry it home. Do not try this yourself!

A twenty-two-year-old Charles Darwin joined the expedition of the HMS *Beagle* in 1831 as the ship's naturalist. Though he was seasick nearly every day for the five years that the *Beagle* sailed, he kept a personal journal, field notebook, and both geological and zoological logbooks for botanical observations. Over the course of that time, he logged meticulous notes about everything he encountered: insects, reptiles, fish, birds, barnacles, bulbs, seeds, shells, jungle life, and coffee plants (which he had never seen growing up in England). He recorded tasting his first banana. He encountered fossils embedded into banks, including the head and bones of a *Megatherium*, which lived millions of years after dinosaurs went extinct, causing him to hypothesize how living animals are connected to extinct creatures.

In 1861, a discovery was made in Germany that provided the "missing link" to Darwin's theory. One of the reptile fossils found there had teeth, claws, and a long tail. But it also had feathers. The *Archaeopteryx*, as it is now called, was the first evidence of how birds evolved from land animals.

Darwin is most famous for the work he did in the Galapagos Islands in the Pacific Ocean, where he collected 5,000 specimens and observed giant tortoises, iguanas, and finches. He observed fourteen different species of finches, which were remarkable for the variety of their beaks, in terms of both shape and how they used them. The beaks, he hypothesized, evolved

Darwin remains a towering figure in the field of evolution for his theory of how species adapt, known as "survival of the fittest."

to accommodate whatever food source was available. It would be another thirty years before Darwin published his groundbreaking book *On the Origin of Species*, which explained how species evolve over the span of generations through their ability to reproduce, developing traits that enable their survival in a changing landscape. My barn swallows had something in common with Darwin's finches: They survived. They were the fittest.

I live in Colorado and travel in and out of the Denver airport quite often. You don't usually associate birds and airports, but it turns out that the inside of airport terminal buildings make hospitable homes. Small birds, such as sparrows, thrive there. I've also seen sparrows in an airport in China! As far as I can tell, the Denver sparrows that nest in the main rotunda have moved in permanently. In all likelihood they were trapped inside when the airport was being built. I've seen birds so bold that they'll hop around the food areas and close to the gates waiting for dropped crumbs. The humans don't bother the sparrows, and the sparrows don't bother the humans. I wonder what would happen if the birds were forced to live outdoors, if they would still have the skills or instincts to survive.

Birds near runways can create huge problems at airports. They can cause severe damage to airplanes and have caused airplane crashes. There is the the famous 2009 flight where Captain Chesley "Sully" Sullenberger landed a large passenger plane on New York City's Hudson River after both engines completely failed. Everybody on the flight survived. The cause of the engine failure was Canada geese sucked into both engines. To discourage birds from nesting on the grass by runways, it is mowed really short. Sometimes border collies are used to chase birds away from the grass strips near runways.

Birds need four basic things: food, water, shelter, and a place to lay their eggs. Birds pretty much like all bodies of water, including ponds, lakes, rivers, and reservoirs. I've seen birds drink from puddles. For most common backyard birds in North America, such as the goldfinch, blue jay, robin, hummingbird, cardinal, and sparrow, their diet consists of nuts, seeds, fruit, and nectar. Ospreys, large coastal birds, like fish and will plunge into the water to scoop them up. Up the food chain: herons like frogs, roadrunners like reptiles, hawks will eat other birds, owls like rodents, and vultures will eat just about anything, including roadkill.

PROJECT #3
PINECONE BIRDFEEDER

You'll need:

- String
- Pinecone (If you don't live near pine trees, you can buy a pinecone at a local crafts store.)
- Birdseed (can be purchased at a grocery or pet store)
- Plate
- Honey
- Butter knife (optional)
- Branch or other place to hang feeder

1. TIE A STRING AROUND A PINECONE'S TOP SO YOU CAN HANG IT UP LATER.

2. POUR ABOUT AN INCH OF BIRDSEED ON A PLATE, ENOUGH TO ROLL YOUR PINECONE IN.

3. DRIZZLE HONEY OVER YOUR PINECONE. (DO THIS OVER THE PLATE TO CATCH ANY HONEY THAT DRIPS OFF YOUR PINECONE.)

4. ONCE YOUR PINECONE IS COVERED IN HONEY, ROLL IT AROUND IN BIRDSEED ON YOUR PLATE UNTIL IT IS COVERED. YOU MAY NEED TO USE A BUTTER KNIFE TO GET INTO THE NOOKS AND CRANNIES.

5. HANG YOUR PINECONE FROM A BRANCH AND MOVE A SAFE DISTANCE AWAY TO OBSERVE THE BIRDS THAT COME TO DINE.

The pigeon is another bird that has made its home in airports. Pigeons prefer covered structures, like the parking garage, which is good for them but not great for travelers, as the pigeons tend to poop on cars. During many walks through parking garages at the Denver airport, I observed how pigeon behavior changed between day and night. During the day, I could see a row of heads, and during the night, I could see a row of rear tail feathers.

Pigeons have a long history of living among humans. Originally known as rock doves, they lived on rocky coasts in Europe and the Middle East. We know that they have been used for food for thousands of years. When they were introduced into North America in the 1600s, they were already city dwellers and were quite comfortable setting up homes on building ledges and windowsills, in parks and under bridges.

They are monogamous, meaning they mate for life, and both parents help in raising the chicks. Once they have found a place for their nest, they will often use it over and over. Pigeons have moved into every city in America. Like people, they tend to settle in. Pigeons are more than happy to live off street scraps and don't need much water. Because they can carry diseases and their poop can really mess up buildings and windshields, they are sometimes called "rats with wings."

Pigeons are also known for something else: remarkable navigations skills. A pigeon can travel 1,300 miles and find its way back to where it started. The military has used messenger pigeons in times of war because they were considered the most effective way to communicate over long distances. Sea captains used to keep pigeons

A pigeon perching on the Empire State Building in New York City.

on board, setting them free when they needed help finding land.

In Jennifer Ackerman's book *The Genius of Birds*, she describes bird intelligence as multifaceted: it encompasses the ability to find routes around the world, copy complex songs, and hide thousands of seeds and remember where they are hidden. Birds are also toolmakers and have complex social structures, meaning they are able to reason and can learn from one another. And, of course, they can fly. Ackerman visits the labs of ornithologists (bird scientists) to understand how birds can do all these complex things, especially with tiny brains. She learned that the location of the neurons (nerve cells that transmit signals to other nerve cells) in the brain is more important than how many there are, and also that the kind of nerve circuits an animal has, which determines how it can communicate, is hugely important as well.

Ackerman also points out that birds are often better at navigating than humans. Some scientists believe they use a "map and compass" strategy that combines a sense of direction with an ability to use landmarks to chart the way. "The whole system," she writes, "including both map and compass, appears to consist of multiple elements involving different types of information—sun, stars, magnetic fields, landscape features, wind and weather." Scientists have been tracking birds' migratory patterns (called flyways) to learn about their internal GPS. Some have even conducted studies by strapping tiny geolocaters (global location sensors) to birds to research their routes. In other words, we really do not know how they do it. But we really want to find out.

A FEATHER IN HER CAP

Florence Merriam Bailey was not pleased. Many women in the late 1800s wore hats with elaborate decorations, including feathers and sometimes little stuffed birds. To keep up with demand, hat companies were killing birds in huge numbers. This horrified Bailey, who had loved birds from the time she was young. At Smith College, she formed a local Audubon Society, taking her classmates on nature walks and introducing them to the individual beauty of different kinds of birds. She thought if she could share the wondrous beauty of birds, women would be less likely to use them for hat decoration. The National Audubon Society had just been formed by two women with the same goal of stopping the hunting and trading of birds. Their pioneering work led to the Weeks-McLean Law, which outlawed hunting birds for market and forbade selling birds across state lines.

Bailey's first book, *Birds Through an Opera-Glass*, was among the first to popularize the science of birds. Opera glasses were invented around the same time as binoculars, which made close-up bird watching possible. Her book *Birds of the of Western United States*, published in 1902, was the first to describe birds in their natural habitat. She also wrote about their behaviors: nesting, feeding, and birdsong. Her contribution to bird science earned her the honor of becoming the first woman allowed into the American Ornithologists' Union.

When I was around eight years old, my siblings and I noticed a robin's nest just outside our living room window. On closer inspection, the nest had three or four tiny blue eggs inside. We were eager to explore, but our mother warned us not to disturb the nest. She told us that the mother might not return if she feared predators (us!) were near. We hadn't thought of ourselves as predators, but we would never risk scaring the mother away from her chicks. Instead, we'd quietly approach the window from inside the living room and peer into the nest a few times a day. For the first two weeks, the mother incubated the eggs, warming them with her body heat. She left a few times but only for a few minutes. When the eggs finally hatched, the babies looked like prehistoric creatures with their wet feathers and enormous beaks opening and closing in hopes of getting a bit of worm or berry. We watched as the mother returned with food for the chicks. The nestlings competed for food by "begging," sort of like a bunch of siblings fighting for the biggest piece of pizza or cake. What I didn't know was that the birds were eating regurgitated (pre-chewed) food! Of course, it makes sense. We humans mash up food for our babies, too—though most parents don't pre-chew it!

Around twelve days later, the biggest chick perched on the edge of the nest and flew! Its nearly translucent skin and soft down had transformed into wings. The other chicks followed over the next day or two. I couldn't imagine those tiny birds surviving on their own. But unlike a human baby, which takes a year before it learns to walk (and still needs constant supervision), a nestling becomes independent at four weeks.

Once the robin and her babies were gone, my mother said it was okay to get the nest. We tore off and were surprised to find what we did. From our window view, it looked as if the nest was made of twigs. But on closer inspection, the cup-shaped nest also had bits of paper, feathers, moss, and a piece of blue twine that looked like what the paperboy used to tie up the stacks of newspapers. The whole thing was cemented by mud, and the inside was lined with soft grass. It also smelled awful! It made sense. The birds had nested, been birthed, and pooped in the nest! No wonder they leave it for good when the chicks are ready to fly.

PROJECT # 4
BUILD A NEST

Birds make nests out of whatever materials they can find in their environment. Often that means twigs and branches, but it can also include a bird's own feathers, or man-made elements, like the paper and twine I found in the robin's nest outside my childhood home.

You'll need:
- Twigs
- Grass, twine, and/or string
- Mud

INSTRUCTIONS

1. START BY BUILDING A BASE WITH THE BIGGER TWIGS. THE BASE SHOULD BE THE SIZE OF YOUR HAND.

2. BUILD UP THE WALLS BY ADDING LAYER AFTER LAYER OF TWIGS.

3. WITH EACH LAYER, WEAVE IN STRING, LONG PIECES OF GRASS, AND/OR TWINE TO HOLD THE WALLS IN PLACE.

4. THEN USE YOUR MUD AS SPACKLE (PASTE TO FILL IN THE HOLES AND CRACKS). EXPERIMENT WITH THE CONSISTENCY OF THE MUD. YOU MIGHT NEED WETTER MUD TO FILL IN GAPS AND DRIER CONSISTENCY TO BUILD THE WALLS.

5. WHEN THE WALLS ARE 3-4 INCHES HIGH, LINE YOUR NEST WITH SOFT GRASS. NOW YOU KNOW WHAT IT'S LIKE TO BE A BIRD, BUILDING YOUR HOME.

There are more varieties of birds' nests than human dwellings. Can you imagine building a house out of your own saliva? That is exactly what the Southeast Asian edible-nest swiftlets do. During mating season, the male swiftlet secretes a special kind of saliva that he uses to build a nest on the upper wall of a cave. The Asian tailorbird is named for its ability to sew. It pokes holes in leaves and threads them with insect silk to pull the leaves together into a nest. The native African sociable weaver finds safety in numbers by building massive communal nests that look like someone dropped a haystack onto a tree. These nests are the largest in the animal kingdom and can sometimes house up to 100 weaver couples and weigh several tons. North American ovenbirds build their dome nests out of dead leaves, grass, bark, and animal hair

Wikimedia Commons/Sara&Joachim

from the forest floor. They look like tiny pizza ovens with a round opening. And some birds don't build nests at all. King penguins will incubate an egg by holding it between their legs, the males and females alternating between who holds the egg and who hunts for food.

The native African sociable weavers' massive communal nest—an incredible collaborative feat.

In many bird species, the male will build a nest as part of the courting ritual. If a female is impressed with the male's nest, she will mate with him. But nests not only need to impress potential mates, they need to keep eggs safe from predators. The female great hornbill goes to extraordinary lengths to protect her young, sealing herself inside a tree cavity with mud to lay and incubate her eggs while relying on her mate to feed her through a tiny hole. In China, I saw birds nesting on big electrical towers, and in my home state of Colorado, I spied an eagle nest on an electrical tower as well. They figured out how to build a flat triangular structure on the cross struts. It's a pretty safe bet no human is going to mess with those birds.

PROJECT #5
BUILD A BIRD FEEDER

You'll need:
- Empty half-gallon milk carton or jug
- Scissors
- 1 dowel long enough to go through the carton with two inches left on either side
- Craft paint, markers, glue, bark, twigs (optional)
- String or wire
- Branch or other place to hang birdhouse
- Birdseed

INSTRUCTIONS

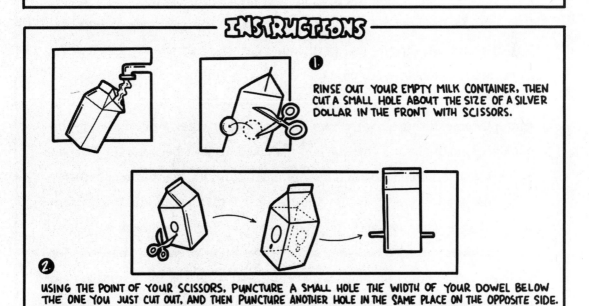

❶ RINSE OUT YOUR EMPTY MILK CONTAINER, THEN CUT A SMALL HOLE ABOUT THE SIZE OF A SILVER DOLLAR IN THE FRONT WITH SCISSORS.

❷ USING THE POINT OF YOUR SCISSORS, PUNCTURE A SMALL HOLE THE WIDTH OF YOUR DOWEL BELOW THE ONE YOU JUST CUT OUT, AND THEN PUNCTURE ANOTHER HOLE IN THE SAME PLACE ON THE OPPOSITE SIDE. SLIDE IN YOUR DOWEL THROUGH THESE HOLES. THE DOWEL SHOULD STICK OUT A COUPLE OF INCHES ON BOTH SIDES. THIS WILL MAKE A PERCH FOR BIRDS ON BOTH SIDES OF THE HOUSE, AS WELL AS ON THE INSIDE.

(CONTINUED)

③ DECORATE YOUR BIRDHOUSE, REMEMBERING IT WILL BE SUBJECT TO RAIN AND OTHER WEATHER. SOME IDEAS INCLUDE GLUING ON BARK, TWIGS, OR LEAVES, OR PAINTING PICTURES OF BIRDS ON IT.

④ PUNCTURE TWO MORE HOLES IN THE TOP OF YOUR MILK CONTAINER THE WIDTH OF YOUR STRING. RUN ENOUGH STRING OR WIRE THROUGH TO HANG YOUR BIRDHOUSE. FIND A SAFE LOCATION, LIKE A STURDY BRANCH, AND HANG UP YOUR HOUSE.

POLLY WANT A CRACKER?

Irene M. Pepperberg was four years old when her father gave her a parakeet. That gift would begin a lifelong love of birds. In her memoir, *Alex & Me*, Irene tells how she was influenced by the children's book *The Story of Doctor Dolittle* by Hugh Lofting. Dr. Dolittle preferred treating animals to humans. This spoke to the shy and awkward young girl who had already developed a closer relationship with her parakeets than with kids her own age. She began to teach her parakeet how to speak, or in any case how to mimic her. One triumph came during a high school chemistry class when a bird flew into the lab. Everyone, including the teacher, panicked, in part because the Bunsen burners were on. Irene instructed everyone to turn off their burners and stay calm. She got a saucer of water, and the bird settled down and drank from the bowl, giving her a chance to catch the bird and release it back outside.

Though Pepperberg had long planned to study chemistry, her love for birds led her to study animal cognition instead, which is the scientific field that studies whether and how animals think. Scientists disagree about animal thought. Some scientists think that only humans are capable of complex thought, while other scientists believe that some very advanced animals (like chimpanzees and dolphins) can think as well. Few people believed that any birds were capable of complex thought.

In 1977, Irene bought an African gray parrot with a mission to see whether her bird, which she called Alex, was capable of thought. Pepperberg taught Alex to identify 50 objects and to speak about 150 words. Though many parrots can "speak," they are only imitating human speech and don't understand what the words mean. Alex was different. He appeared to understand concepts like bigger/smaller and same/different. If you asked him how many red blocks were on a tray, he could answer accurately, even if the tray contained objects of other colors and shapes. Alex learned a number of phrases to express his desires, such as "I'm sorry," "Want nut," and "Wanna go back," meaning he wanted to go back to his cage. Scientists are still debating whether Alex was just "vocalizing" or if he was demonstrating something more complex, but either way, he brought us a little closer to understanding birds. When Alex died at the early age of thirty-one (African grays can often live up to sixty years in captivity), his last words to Irene were, "You be good. I love you."

Courtesy of Arlene Levin

Irene Pepperberg working with Alex.

I'm awakened almost every morning at 5:00 a.m. by a symphony of birds outside my window. Scientists don't agree on why birds vocalize more in the morning, but one theory is that the male birds are announcing their health and dominance, which makes them more attractive to the females. They also may sing in the morning to ward off other birds or predators, protecting their territory. Not all birds are songbirds. Some birds make a call instead of a song. A call is instinctive, but a songbird learns much the way humans learn language: they imitate the "adults."

You can try "talking" to birds by imitating their calls, or whistling. Many birds, such as songbirds and starlings, are capable of mimicking sounds. Another way to whistle: Try putting a blade of grass (as wide as possible) between the base and top of your thumbs, holding it as taut as possible. Then put it up to your mouth and blow.

If you're walking in the woods in pursuit of spotting birds, do not wear white or bright colors. Unlike some other animals, birds can see the full color spectrum. (Fun fact: dogs and horses cannot see the color red.) You want to camouflage or disappear as much as possible so as not to scare the birds. I once was taking a hike and got a very funny feeling. What I thought was a tree stepped forward and scared me half to death. It was a birder camouflaged to look like bark.

When birding, you want to stay very quiet and still so that once you spot your bird, it doesn't fly away. Because the next step is where the interesting part begins. Identifying your bird requires that you observe four key features:

- Size/shape
- Color pattern
- Behavior
- Habitat

Is your bird tiny, small, medium, large, or huge? With respect to its features: Does your bird have long, skinny legs? Is your bird sleek or chubby? What shape beak does it have? What color is your bird? If it's yellow, is it the same yellow on the entire bird or does it fade out? Are there any markings, such as streaks, spots, or a different-colored crown or tail? Last, what can you determine about the bird's habitat and behavior? What kind of nest (if you can find the nest) does it live in? Does it live in the forest or by the shore? Does it sing, and if so, what does it sound like? A peep? A tweet? A chirp or a warble? There are a few free apps to help with bird identification, including birdsong, such as the Merlin Bird ID by Cornell Lab. You can also use what people have been using for centuries: field guides.

BIRDS OF A FEATHER

Though Florence Merriam Bailey introduced what we think of as the modern field guide drawn from nature, she was not alone in furthering the art and science of bird observation. John James Audubon (he didn't start the Audubon Society, but they did name it after him) was born in 1785. He started drawing birds and eggs from the time he was a child. He is credited with performing the first bird-banding study in the United States. He attached strings to the talons of eastern phoebes, small gray birds. The following year, Audubon recognized the birds by the strings on their feet and concluded that the birds return to the same nesting grounds every year. At the age of thirty-five, Audubon vowed to paint every bird in America. Unable to sell his work in the United

James Audubon saw his first American flamingo in 1832 on the southeast coast of Florida. This is plate number 431 in his set of paintings.

States, he went to London, where his paintings were met with much enthusiasm. A publisher recognized the beauty of his work and agreed to print his paintings. The life-sized colored engravings depict 489 species of bird. Today, 120 complete sets of the original printings exist. They are mostly in libraries and museums, but in 2000, one was sold at auction for 8.8 million dollars, a record for any book at the time.

Roger Tory Peterson had skipped two grades in school, and as a result the older kids sometimes teased him, calling him "Professor Nuts Peterson" because of his love of nature. Little did they realize that his passion and talent would shape the way generations of birders would understand birdlife. His particular talent for drawing birds was evident at seventeen when two of his drawings were displayed at major bird exhibitions alongside work by experts in the field. In 1934, he published a field guide to birds that's still accompanying bird-watchers on nature walks. Eighty years later, it's considered the first modern field guide and helped popularize bird-watching in America. A key feature: you could hold it in your hand, which meant you could take it into the field. But it was more than that. Roger Tory Peterson changed the way field guides were organized. Instead of grouping birds in the same family, he put them together according to similarities and used little black arrows to point out common features. This hugely helped birders in their quest to identify birds. He is also remembered for helping inspire what we think of today as environmentalism or the environmental movement.

More recently, David Allen Sibley has been carrying forward the legacies of Audubon and Peterson. By age seven, Sibley was drawing birds. Soon after, he learned to band birds, handling the birds and observing them at close range. His father was an ornithologist at Yale University and exposed his son to every aspect of birdlife. More artist than scientist, he took to his father's world through drawing. As an adult, Sibley illustrated, wrote, and published his wildly successful guide to North American birds, *The Sibley Guide to Birds*. Sibley not only described their natural habitat and behavior, he did something completely new and mind-blowing: he illustrated birds in flight.

PROJECT #6
FIELD GUIDE TO BIRDS

You can create an elaborate or simple field guide. And don't worry if you're not great at drawing—you can always use an existing field guide and trace the bird you plan to draw.

You'll need:

- Pencil
- Ruler
- Drawing notebook
- Binoculars (optional)
- Camera (optional)
- Colored pencils
- Field guide or access to the internet
- Watercolors (optional)
- Tracing paper (optional)

INSTRUCTIONS

1. USING YOUR PENCIL AND RULER, DIVIDE EACH PAGE OF YOUR NOTEBOOK INTO FOUR COLUMNS: SIZE/SHAPE, COLOR PATTERN, HABITAT, AND BEHAVIOR. LEAVE THE BOTTOM HALF OF THE PAGE FOR A SKETCH.

Robin

2. IDENTIFY THE BIRD YOU WANT TO INCLUDE, AND WRITE ITS NAME ON THE TOP OF THE PAGE. IF YOU DON'T YET KNOW WHAT IT IS, LEAVE IT BLANK FOR NOW. (THE WHOLE POINT OF FEILD GUIDES IS TO HELP YOU IDENTIFY BIRDS.)

CLICK!

3. IF YOU HAVE BINOCULARS, STUDY THE BIRD THROUGH THEM. OBSERVING WITH YOUR EYES IS ALSO FINE. IF YOU HAVE A CAMERA, SNAP A FEW PHOTOS, INCLUDING CLOSE-UPS.

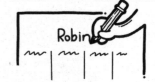

Size
About as big as my hand.

Color
Brown back, red chest, white belly

4. START FILLING IN COLUMNS WITH AS MUCH INFORMATION AS YOU CAN OBSERVE. BE AS SPECIFIC AS POSSIBLE.

5. DRAW YOUR BIRD USING COLORED PENCILS. DON'T WORRY IF YOU'RE NOT A SKILLED ARTIST; YOU CAN START BY TRACING YOUR BIRD FROM A FIELD GUIDE, IF YOU'VE BEEN ABLE TO IDENTIFY IT ALREADY. IF YOU'RE MORE CONFIDENT, APPLY WATERCOLORS TO YOUR SKETCH.

6. IF YOU WEREN'T ABLE TO IDENTIFY IF BEFORE YOU DREW IT, NOW IS TIME TO USE A FIELD GUIDE OR GO ONLINE TO MAKE A POSITIVE IDENTIFICATION OF YOUR BIRD. MOST FIELD GUIDES ARE FOR SPECIFIC REGIONS, SO YOU'LL HAVE TO FIND ONE FOR WHERE YOU LIVE. ONE GREAT ONLINE RESOURCE IS WWW.ALLABOUTBIRDS.ORG/NEWS/

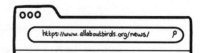

https://www.allaboutbirds.org/news/

To be a birder, all you have to do is go outside. You don't need anything more than your eyes and a bird, and birds are virtually everywhere. But spotting birds is just the beginning. If you decide to get more serious about birding, you'll want to think about the following things. First, where do birds like to hang out? We already know that swallows like the eaves of barns and pigeons like parking garages. If you have a tiny yard or a tree in front of an apartment building, you can make it more hospitable to birds. You can put a bird feeder in a tree, and you can add a birdbath to your yard. It's like throwing a party for the birds with refreshments. You'll get many more species if you provide the snacks.

Beyond your home, go to a city park, a state park, an open field, a forest, or depending where you live, a rain forest. Birds pretty much live in every kind of habitat, including the tundra, the seacoast, and the desert. There are annual competitions among birders to spot the most bird species. The international record goes to Arjan Dwarshius, who spotted 6,852 different species out of 10,000 over the course of one year. Pretty impressive.

For me, I'm happy to hear birdsong outside my window, observe a line of kestrels on an electric wire surveying the fields beyond for food, or watch a single robin or blue jay swoop from one branch to another across the yard in an elegant arc. I take many flights a year, but no matter how much I enjoy the feeling of lifting off into the air and flying, I still wonder what it would be like to soar like a bird.

PROJECT #7
CITIZEN SCIENCE, BIRD AND INSECT POPULATIONS

Populations of many bird species have declined. This is caused by several factors, such as loss of habitat and fewer insects for food. Ken Rosenberg from the Cornell Lab of Ornithology states that birds have declined in North America by 30 percent since 1970. There are a few species that have increased, such as Canada geese. They have adapted well to human activities, such as growing crops and having large lawns. In Colorado, the Canada geese stay all winter and graze on fields and lawns. Unfortunately, the insects that are sources of food for smaller birds have also declined 40 percent. Some of the decline of insects may be due to chemicals. Three-quarters of all plants that have flowers are pollinated by insects. Insects, such as bees, are essential for pollinating one-third of the crops that are grown for food. Here are some ideas for citizen science projects for counting insect and bird populations.

National Geographic has great projects on this topic. You can visit nationalgeographic.org/idea/citizen-science-projects to check them out. The Cornell Lab has fun ideas over at birds.cornell.edu/citizenscience. Head to calacademy.org/citizen-science for ideas from the California Academy of Sciences. The North American Butterfly Association, at naba.org, is another place to look, as is the Audubon Society Christmas Bird Count at audubon.org/conservation/join-christmas-bird-count. And you can take a look at the bibliography at the back of this book (it's on page 179) for even more ideas.

THE NIGHT SKIES

CHAPTER FIVE

I was antsy all through supper. I couldn't wait to be done so that I could run to the field across the street from our house and join the other kids and neighbors who were already there, looking up at the night sky. We had been told to look just after sunset for the famous Russian satellite orbiting Earth. When a bright light appeared in the sky, we all jumped up. Then, deflated, we saw that it was just a plane. This happened a few times. We'd get all excited, then, "No!" False alarm.

I was ten years old when the Soviet Union (which mostly covered what is now Russia) launched the first satellite made by humans to orbit the earth. It was called Sputnik, which translates into English as "fellow traveler," and it was a big deal. Sputnik was the size of a beach ball, weighed 183.9 pounds, and took 98 minutes to complete one orbit (which means one loop around the planet). The satellite was highly reflective and visible from the earth with binoculars or even the naked eye. Rooftop parties across the country gathered to glimpse its flight around the earth. Sputnik was meant to obtain information about meteors, the atmosphere, and radio signals. But most important, it officially started the Space Age, igniting an ongoing competition for dominance of the skies between the two world superpowers: the United States and the Soviet Union. This competition was known as the space race, and the Soviet Union had bested the United States by sending the first satellite around the earth. Humans had conquered land and seas and skies, or at least harnessed their power. Space was the final frontier.

In 1958, a year after Sputnik's launch, the United States Congress passed the National Aeronautics and Space Act, which created the National Aeronautics and Space Administration, also known as NASA. They had one goal in mind: put a man on the moon. When most people think of NASA, they think of the astronauts in their white suits and bubble helmets. But there was an army of people behind those brave men who worked on every aspect of the project, including scientists, engineers, astrophysicists, and experts in information technology, data systems, and planetary studies, to name a few. You can still apply for a job to work at NASA today, but you'll probably need a background in STEM (science, technology, engineering, and math).

PROJECT #1
SPOTTING SATELLITES IN THE SKY

There are many satellites that you can spot from the ground. They have many functions, such as aiding communication, operating GPS, and monitoring weather. Some satellites and the orbiting space stations can be seen without a telescope. Seeing satellites will be easier if you are in a dark place far away from high light pollution. Here are some places to start your search:

- Spot the space station—Joe Rao, "How to Spot Satellites," space.com /6870-spot-satellites.html. This website contains lots of information on when and how to look for a satellite orbiting the earth.
- There is also information on nasa.gov.
- Another alternative is to contact an astronomy professor at a local university or community college. Many professors are eager to talk to students who are interested in their work and will help you find information about looking for satellites in your area.

ANYTHING YOU CAN DO, I CAN DO BETTER

"I counted everything. I counted the steps to the road, the steps up to church, the number of dishes and silverware I washed . . . anything that could be counted, I did." Katherine Johnson was wired for math since she was very young. But growing up in her town in West Virginia in the 1920s meant that education was not available to Black people past the eighth grade. Johnson's parents moved 120 miles to find another school for their brilliant daughter where her abilities would flourish. She graduated high school at fourteen. By the time she graduated from college at the age of eighteen, she had taken every math class available and earned grades that put her at the top of her class. She attended graduate school when it was still uncommon for universities to allow Black students to enroll, let alone Black women. Even with these incredible accomplishments, the only mathematics career open to Black women was that of schoolteacher. And that's what Johnson did. What changed the course of her life changed the course of history.

Langley Memorial Aeronautical Laboratory first opened its doors to white women, and then Black women, during World War II when men fighting overseas created a labor shortage at home. With the space race on the horizon, Langley needed as many qualified workers as they could get, and Johnson jumped at the opportunity. Entry-level jobs were opening for positions called "human computers." These positions required computing complex calculations that, before the invention of the digital computer, needed to be performed by humans. Johnson and her fellow mathematicians did their work with pencils and slide rules, which look like rulers with movable parts that can calculate distances, do multiplication, and find the square root of a number.

Johnson joined Langley when segregation in the South was enforced, which meant that Black people were not allowed the rights of full citizens, including being barred from using the same facilities and bathrooms as white people. Despite the discrimination leveled at Black women, Johnson's abilities earned her a promotion first to aerospace technologist, and then to the special task force that successfully launched the first American-piloted orbital mission around the earth. Johnson's calculations were so highly regarded that astronaut John Glenn trusted her work over the digital computers. He famously said, "Get the girl to check the numbers."

Johnson commented that while everyone was focused on getting the men into space, she was focused on getting them home.

If the flight trajectory was too steep, the module that the astronauts were in would burst into flames. If it was too shallow, it would skip off the surface of the atmosphere and drift off into outer space. But John Glenn returned home safely. Her figures worked.

Johnson's story and the story of the women who worked alongside her were largely forgotten until Margot Lee Shetterly

Photo courtesy of NASA

NASA mathematician Katherine Johnson at her desk at the Langley Research Center. Her calculations helped put men into space and on the moon.

published a book called *Hidden Figures*, which later became a popular movie. I never would have known about Katherine Johnson without the book and movie. At ninety-seven, Johnson received the Presidential Medal of Freedom from President Obama. History is incomplete without these stories.

Twelve years after Sputnik's launch, America made the thrilling breakthrough of sending three men to the moon: Neil Armstrong and Buzz Aldrin walked on the moon while Michael Collins stayed in the command module *Columbia* orbiting the moon. When Armstrong first stepped onto the moon's surface, he marked the accomplishment with what is probably one of the best-known quotes in the world: "That's one small step for man, one giant leap for mankind." I was interning at a research lab at the time, and we all gathered around the TV to watch the launch, staring at the fuzzy black-and-white pictures. Six hundred million people around the world watched those same images of Armstrong planting the American flag on the moon. It was mind-blowing. When I got home that night, I walked outside and looked up at the moon, saying with astonishment, "There are people walking around up there."

On the moon, the astronauts found mountains, craters, and flat surfaces covered by the hardened remains of ancient lava flows. We already knew a great deal about the moon's relationship to Earth, including that the moon takes 27.3 days to orbit the earth and doesn't emit any light of its own. We can see the moon because it reflects light from the sun. When the earth is between the moon and the sun, we see a full moon. As the moon moves around the earth, we can see more or less of its surface, which is known as waxing and waning.

Photo courtesy of NASA

Earthrise as seen from the moon, taken by Apollo 8 *astronaut Bill Anders during the 1968 mission.*

The eight phases of the moon: new moon, waxing crescent, first quarter, waxing gibbous, full, waning gibbous, third quarter, and waning crescent.

PROJECT #2
— PHASES OF THE MOON —

You'll need:

- Ruler
- 1 piece of 8 ½" x 11" (80-lb.) black cardstock
- Jar lid with a 2 ½" diameter
- Pencil
- Scissors
- 1 piece of 5" x 11" (80-lb.) white cardstock

INSTRUCTIONS

1. USE THE RULER TO PRECISELY FOLD THE SHEET OF BLACK CARDSTOCK IN HALF LENGTHWISE.

2. USING THE JAR LID AND PENCIL, DRAW A CIRCLE IN THE MIDDLE OF THE BOTTOM PORTION OF THE FOLDED SHEET OF PAPER. USING YOUR SCISSORS, CUT THE CIRCLE OUT.

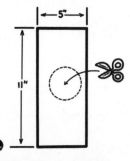

3. USING THE JAR LID AND PENCIL, DRAW A CIRCLE IN THE MIDDLE OF THE WHITE SHEET OF CARDSTOCK. USING YOUR SCISSORS, CUT THE CIRCLE OUT.

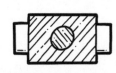

4. TAKE THE REMAINING PIECE OF CARDTOCK (THE PART WITH THE CIRCLE CUT OUT) AND PLACE IT INSIDE THE FOLDED SHEET OF BLACK CARDSTOCK SO THAT THE TWO CUT-OUT CIRCLES LINE UP. YOU SHOULD HAVE WHITE CARDSTOCK STICKING OUT OF THE SIDES OF THE BLACK CARDSTOCK AND ONLY BE ABLE TO SEE A BLACK CIRCLE. THIS IS A NEW MOON.

5. TO VIEW YOUR LUNAR CYCLE, PULL THE LEFT SIDE OF THE WHITE CARDSTOCK SLOWLY TO THE LEFT. A SMALL SLIVER OF WHITE ON THE RIGHT-HAND SIDE REPRESENTS THE WAXING CRESCENT. USING THE IMAGE BELOW, CREATE ALL EIGHT CYCLES OF THE MOON'S PHASE'S.

It took a tremendous amount of innovation and dedication to achieve the dream of sending a man to the moon. New technologies had to be developed to equip the rockets with things like heat shields so that the rocket could reenter the atmosphere without burning up and flight equipment that could both launch the space module into orbit and return it safely. They had to figure out how to supply the astronauts with food, air, and bathrooms! Another important advance in technology that enabled the lunar module *Eagle* to land on the moon was something called variable thrust. Thrust is the force that gets aircraft into the air. Variable thrust is a fancy term for varying the speed on a rocket. It acts like brakes on a car, enabling the spaceship to slow down. Without this new technology, the module would not have had the control necessary to hover over the surface of the moon and land on it.

The space suits worn by the astronauts also presented technical challenges that had never been faced before. NASA had a contest to find the best engineering company to design the space suits. The criteria were that the suit had to protect the astronauts from extreme temperatures and environments, supply oxygen, have an adjustable "thermostat" to control the temperature inside the suit, and be able to inflate and pressurize so the astronauts could breathe. One key feature of the suit was its flexibility, giving the astronauts freedom of movement so they could shift around the cabin, work the controls, and be able to walk when they landed on the moon. The winner of the competition was completely unexpected. Instead of a leading engineering firm, the finest bra and girdle manufacturer won the contract with its hand-sewn space suits. Employing their expert seamstresses, Playtex had every suit hand-sewn using the flexible materials, such as latex, they used for bras and girdles!

One of the greatest innovations that came out of the space program was the computer chip. The computer in the lunar lander is the ancestor to every laptop and mobile phone today. By today's standards, it was a bulky 70 pounds, but that is still tiny compared to the refrigerator-sized mainframes that were used to store data back then. The computing power in the lunar lander was equal to the first Apple computers. To give you a sense of how basic the lunar lander's computer was, a multifunction hand calculator had more power. I was appalled to learn that the computer on board *Apollo 11* crashed during the first lunar landing: the computer screen went blank for a full ten seconds. Ten seconds may not seem like a lot, but it can be a matter of life and death when you're on the moon. To reduce the load on the computer's tiny memory, the astronauts switched off the antenna that connected them with the orbiting spacecraft. What saved the mission was a new program that automatically kicked in and saved the navigation data.

It was a little-known computer scientist from MIT named Hal Laning who figured out how to reboot the computer while the module kept flying. His equations were the basis of *Apollo 11*'s guidance computer. "Much of the work was done by others," he said, "but I supplied the basic concept, the basic equations." Without his contribution, the landing might not have happened. Stephen Witt writes in *Wired* magazine that "Aldrin and Armstrong got the glory, but housed in a metal box on the back wall of the lander was the blueprint for the modern world."

PROJECT #3
MODEL ROCKET

You'll need:

- 2-liter soda bottle
- Duct tape
- 3 unsharpened pencils
- Cork that will fit in the

- neck of the soda bottle
- Baking soda
- Measuring spoons
- 1 square of toilet paper

- White vinegar
- Glass jar at least 5" tall
- Funnel

INSTRUCTIONS

1. TO CREATE YOUR ROCKET FINS (STAND), TURN YOUR SODA BOTTLE UPSIDE DOWN AND DUCT TAPE YOUR THREE PENCILS TO THE BOTTLE (ERASER END ON THE GROUND) SO THAT THE OPEN END OF THE BOTTLE IS APPROXIMATELY 2½ INCHES FROM THE GROUND. THE PENCILS SHOULD BE EVENLY SPACED AROUND THE BOTTLE. THE BOTTLE SHOULD BE ABLE TO STAND FIRMLY ON THE GROUND ONCE THE PENCILS ARE ATTACHED.

2.5"

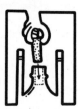

2. TEST YOUR CORK BY INSERTING IT INTO THE BOTTLE, MAKING SURE IT FITS SNUGLY, BUT NOT FIRMLY. IF YOU HAVE TO FORCE THE CORK INSIDE THE BOTTLE TOP, IT WILL NOT LAUNCH AS WELL.

3. CREATE YOUR BAKING SODA PACKET BY PLACING 1 TEASPOON OF BAKING SODA IN THE MIDDLE OF THE SQUARE OF TOILET PAPER. FOLD TIGHTLY SO THE BAKING SODA REMAINS IN THE PACKET WHEN PLACED IN THE BOTTLE.

4. FLIP YOUR BOTTLE SO IT IS NECK SIDE UP. PREPARE YOUR "ROCKET FUEL" BY PLACING 6 TABLESPOONS OF VINEGAR INTO A SEPARATE JAR.

5. GENTLY PLACE THE PACKET OF BAKING SODA INSIDE THE BOTTLE. USING THE FUNNEL, POUR YOUR JAR OF VINEGAR INTO THE BOTTLE.

6 WORKING QUICKLY, PRESS THE CORK INTO THE BOTTLE OPENING AND FLIP THE BOTTLE OVER SO IT IS STANDING ON ITS FINS. THE MIXTURE WILL BEGIN TO FOAM.

7 STEP BACK AND WAIT FOR LIFTOFF!

Today, stargazing isn't as easy as it used to be. The main reason is light pollution. When we think of pollution, we tend to focus on things like water and air pollution because they directly affect what we drink and breathe. But light pollution has long interfered with our ability to see the night skies in cities and suburbs. Sixty years ago growing up in suburban Massachusetts, I could just look up at the sky and see stars and planets. My grandfather pointed out the various constellations. He showed me how to find the North Star by lining up the stars in the Big Dipper and making a straight line to the brightest star at the end of the Little Dipper's handle. The North Star has been guiding sailors and travelers for hundreds of years.

It was at my aunt's ranch in Arizona where I first saw a star-filled sky

Photo courtesy NASA Earth Observatory

This composite image of the United States shows the regions with the highest concentration of light pollution.

against what looked like a blanket of black velvet. Every star shined brilliantly. I was captivated by the beauty and thought about how big the universe was. I think it's good from time to time to take stock of how insignificant we are—and I mean that in a good way.

TRACKING LIGHT POLLUTION

An exciting citizen science project that you can participate in involves capturing the night sky from where you live and sharing it with people across the globe to track light pollution.

You can find directions for how to do this on the website Globe at Night: globeatnight.org/6-steps.php.

The night skies have always been important to humankind, primarily as a navigational tool. Once people realized that stars always show up in certain parts of the sky at certain times of the year, we could navigate according to the positions of the stars and planets. Ancient civilizations recognized that the patterns in the night sky appeared again and again, each civilization interpreting the stars in their own way. Some believed the stars could be used to tell the future, while others saw representations of mythical figures. People also used the stars to keep track of the seasons, which helped them plant and harvest at the best times. Most civilizations developed calendars, often based around the phases of the moon.

CONNECTING THE DOTS

In 1608, a Dutch glasses maker invented something that would change the course of astronomy. Hans Lippershey created the telescope and was granted the patent to his invention. It gave us the first look into the night skies and enlarged our view of the universe and our place in it. One year later, in 1609, the Italian astronomer

Galileo would improve the telescope to make it more powerful. As a result, he discovered four moons circling around Jupiter, which definitively proved that at least some objects didn't revolve around the earth.

Until then, most people believed that celestial bodies could orbit only the earth. Galileo's observation confirmed the theory of Nicolaus Copernicus, a mathematician and astronomer, who sixty years earlier introduced the idea of heliocentrism, which stated that the earth revolved around the sun. Copernicus didn't publish his findings until his death for fear that his ideas would not be well received. He was correct. In the seventeenth century, if you believed that the earth revolved around the sun, you could be arrested and jailed for life, which is what happened to Galileo. The Catholic church believed that the earth was the center of the world and declared Galileo a heretic, which is basically anyone who went against the beliefs of the church.

The next major contribution toward our understanding of the laws that governed the planets came from seventeenth-century German astronomer Johannes Kepler, whose three laws of planetary motion showed that planets do not orbit around the sun in perfect circles but in oval-like ellipses. As a result, we could make more accurate predictions of how planets move, showing how the sun controls the motion of the planets.

In 1687, Sir Isaac Newton, another giant in the world of science, building on the work of Copernicus, Galileo, and Kepler, published his theory of gravitation and laws of motion, which ultimately proved correct Kepler's laws of planetary motion. In case you were wondering, these laws explain why planets don't fall out of the sky.

PROJECT #5
CONSTELLATION MAPS

You'll need:

- Flashlight
- Drawing compass
- 2 pieces of 8 ½" x 11" (80-lb.) black cardstock
- Pencil

- Scissors
- Tape (optional)
- Pictures of constellations (either online or in a book)

INSTRUCTIONS

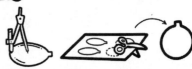

1. MEASURE THE CIRCUMFERENCE OF YOUR FLASHLIGHT'S LENS WITH A DRAWING COMPASS. COPY THE MEASURMEN ONTO CARDSTOCK WITH YOUR PENCIL.

2. CUT OUT A FEW CIRCLES FOR DIFFERENT CONSTELLATIONS. THESE SHOULD FIT SNUGGLY OVER THE LENS AND INSIDE THE LIP OF THE FLASHLIGHT (IF YOUR FLASHLIGHT DOESN'T HAVE A LIP, YOU CAN USE TAPE TO HOLD IT IN PLACE.) IT IS IMPORTANT TO LEAVE A TAB ON THE CIRCLE A LITTLE LARGER THAN A PENCIL ERASER TO PULL YOUR CIRCLE OUT OF THE FLASHLIGHT'S RIM.

4. USING YOUR PENCIL, MARK DOTS ON YOUR INDIVIDUAL CIRCLES THAT LOOK LIKE YOUR CONSTELLATION IMAGES.

3. FIND IMAGES OF CONSTELLATIONS ON THE INTERNET OR IN A BOOK ABOUT ASTRONOMY.

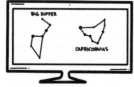

5. USING THE POINTS OF YOUR SCISSORS, PUNCH HOLES THROUGH THE DOTS.

6. INSERT ONE DISC INTO THE TOP OF YOUR FLASHLIGHT. TURN YOUR FLASHLIGHT ON IN A DARK ROOM AND SHINE IT ON A BLANK WALL OR CEILING. ENJOY VIEWING YOUR CONSTELLATION!

In 1997, I was driving home from the Denver airport on Interstate 25 when I saw what looked like an enormous ball up in the sky, followed by streams of light. From the car, it looked stationary. When I got home, I got out of my car to take a closer look. Unfortunately, my view was blocked by the streetlights. It was only visible on the sections of the highway that were totally dark. It was the comet Hale-Bopp, one of the largest comets on record, with a 16- to 26-mile-wide nucleus, which is the comet's center. By comparison, most comets are less than 6 miles wide.

Halley's Comet on its 76-year orbit. You will be able to see it again in 2061! How old will you be then?

Comets are mostly composed of ice with some rock and are sometimes referred to as "dirty snowballs." The most well-known comet is Halley's, named for astronomer Edmond Halley. He used Isaac Newton's law of gravitation and calculated that the comet's orbital path would bring it close to Earth every seventy-six years. Until then, when comets appeared, they were considered a one-time appearance. Though Halley wasn't alive when his comet returned, his math was right, proving that at least some comets orbit the sun. Halley's Comet last made an appearance in 1986. You'll be able to see it again in 2061. People are still identifying new comets to this day, and if you locate one and get approval from the International Astronomical Union, the comet will be named after you.

You've probably heard of the Hubble Space Telescope, though you may not know the man it's named for. Edwin Hubble, an American scientist, is credited with discovering that the universe is filled with galaxies, not just free-floating stars and cosmic gas clouds. His observation changed our view of the universe. The telescope named for him orbits our planet so that its pictures are not distorted by Earth's atmosphere, allowing us to see farther into space than we ever have before.

But it was Robert Williams, then director of the Space Telescope Science Institute, who proposed pointing the Hubble at a dark, completely empty bit of sky near the Big Dipper. People thought it was crazy to spend hours of precious time observing nothing. He was asked, "Why would you look at nothing?" Robert said, "If you are going to make a discovery, you are going to have to be a risk taker." He focused on a tiny patch of sky and took a 100-hour exposure. The image clearly showed that there are thousands of galaxies out there, and the area came to be known as Hubble Deep Field.

The Hubble Space Telescope in orbit on its fifth and final mission in 2009.

Data collected by the Hubble has contributed to over 700,000 scientific papers and our understanding of how old the universe is, how stars form and die, and how galaxies come to exist. The United States is developing an even more powerful telescope that will go beyond the Hubble's capabilities. The James Webb Space Telescope will be better able to detect infrared light and explore the universe's past back to the formation of the first stars and galaxies. And unlike the Hubble, which orbits the earth, the Webb telescope will orbit the sun, about one million miles from Earth.

SPACE CADET

Though he didn't believe in reincarnation, Stephen Hawking loved the fact that he was born three hundred years to the day after the death of Galileo. You could say he was a born scientist. As a young boy, he loved taking apart model trains and airplanes to figure out how they worked. As a teenager, he made a simple computer out of recycled clock and telephone parts. His classmates even nicknamed him "Einstein." He went to University College, Oxford, to study physics and astronomy after rejecting chemistry, biology, and mathematics. He would later explain his decision: "Physics and astronomy offered the hope of understanding where we came from and why we are here."

Hawking is famous for contributing to our understanding of the big bang theory, which posits that the universe had an actual beginning. Until then, scientists believed in a steady state theory, which claimed that the universe always existed without a particular beginning. Hawking showed that a period of rapid expansion, high temperatures, and density resulted in the big bang, the theory now accepted by most scientists.

When Hawking was twenty-one, he was diagnosed with amyotrophic lateral sclerosis, or ALS. The disease affected the nerve cells in his brain and spinal cord, which resulted in Hawking gradually losing control of his muscles and speech, using a wheelchair and necessitating speaking through an electronic sensor. Doctors predicted that Hawking only had a few years left of his life. He defied the odds, living fifty-five years longer than predicted, until the age of seventy-six. Hawking married, had three children, and left his mark on the world.

Photo courtesy of NASA

Hawking living his dream of achieving zero gravity.

Hawking is a personal hero of mine. He never let his disability stop him from living a meaningful life even after he could no longer walk or speak. In an interview with *The New York Times*, Hawking said, "Concentrate on things your disability doesn't prevent you doing well." In 2007, he fulfilled a dream of floating in zero gravity. NASA invited him to board an aircraft that would simulate the weightlessness that astronauts experience in space. Hawking said, "I was Superman for those few minutes."

Do you think aliens or UFOs are real? If you do, you aren't alone. Fifty percent of Americans believe aliens exist, even though we have no evidence at this point. The search for aliens, or extraterrestrial intelligence, is known as SETI. Whether we are alone in the universe, or the only form of intelligent life, is a question scientists, astronomers, astrophysicists, novelists, and filmmakers have always grappled with. No matter how many stories we create attempting to imagine a connection between ourselves and a civilization from another galaxy, we've yet to see any hard evidence of extraterrestrial life. An Italian American physicist named Enrico Fermi believed that if there were other galactic civilizations in existence, we would already know about them. His observation is known as the Fermi paradox, and he is quoted as saying, "So where is everybody?"

I was so caught up in sci-fi and the idea of aliens when I was in boarding school that I pulled off the best hoax my high school had ever witnessed. Using a homemade flying saucer, a fishing pole, and some expert timing, I set out to see if I could fool two of the girls in our dorm into believing that they had seen a real flying saucer. Once I had my flying saucer assembled, I tied it to the end of a fishing rod with some black wire and waited until lights out. Then I climbed up to the roof of my dormitory and positioned myself above the girls' window. I knew if I dangled the flying saucer in front of the window, they would be able to see it clearly and realize it was a model. I also knew if I flew it back and forth too much it would be obvious that the saucer wasn't real. The trick was to not overdo it. I used all my self-restraint and swung the saucer just once in front of the window. I knew my dorm mates had fallen for it when I heard them scream. They had the whole school believing they had seen a flying saucer, and the local newspaper ran an article about the incident. I don't know how I kept quiet the whole time. It wasn't until the end of the year that I dug into the back of my closet and said I had a present for them, handing them the tinfoil saucer. They were mad at first, but it was a harmless prank and everyone thought it was hilarious.

You'll need:

- Scissors
- 2 round paper plates
- Electrical or duct tape
- Newspaper
- Small battery-operated light
- Foil
- Stapler (optional)
- Plastic dome like the kind that comes as a cover for soft-serve ice cream
- Black wire
- Fishing pole or long dowel or rod

INSTRUCTIONS

① USE YOUR SCISSORS TO CUT A 1½-INCH HOLE IN THE CENTER OF ONE OF THE PAPER PLATES.

② HOLD THE PLATES TOGETHER SO THAT THE RIMS ARE FACING EACH OTHER, AND THEN ATTACH THEM WITH TAPE AROUND HALF OF THEIR CIRCUMFERENCE.

③ FILL THE TAPED SECTION WITH CRUNCHED NEWSPAPER SO THAT IT MAKES A SAUCER SHAPE.

④ INSTALL YOUR LIGHT IN THE CENTER SO THAT THE BULB COMES OUT OF THE HOLE.

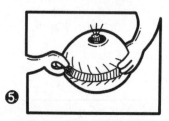

⑤ STUFF THE REST OF THE PLATE WITH NEWSPAPER AND TAPE THE REST OF THE CIRCUMFERENCE SO THAT IT'S COMPLETELY SEALED.

⑥ COVER THE DISC WITH FOIL. YOU MAY NEED TO STAPLE AROUND THE EDGES TO KEEP THE FOIL IN PLACE.

⑦ TAPE THE PLASTIC DOME OVER THE HOLE ON ONE SIDE SO THAT THE TAPE BECOMES A HINGE. YOU MAY NEED TO CUT ONE SIDE OF THE DOME INTO A STRAIGHT EDGE SO THAT THE DOME WILL HINGE MORE EASILY.

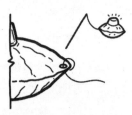

⑧ MAKE A HOLE WITH YOUR SCISSORS NEAR THE RIM AND THREAD THE WIRE THROUGH. DEPENDING ON WHERE YOU INTEND TO FLY THE SAUCER, ADJUST THE LENGTH ACCORDINGLY. WRAP THE END OF YOUR WIRE AROUND THE DOWEL.

⑨ WHEN YOU ARE READY TO FREAK OUT A SIBLING, PARENT, OR FRIEND, TURN ON THE LIGHT, AND THEN TAPE DOWN THE OTHER SIDE OF THE DOME. SWING IT **ONCE** IN FRONT OF A WINDOW WHEN YOU KNOW THEY ARE THERE. FOR BEST RESULTS, FLY YOUR SAUCER AT NIGHT.

A STAR IS BORN

When the young Carl Sagan wanted to learn about the stars, his mother sent him to the library. According to biographer Keay Davidson, Sagan asked the librarian for a book about stars and she brought him one with pictures of movie stars. *Oops.* Embarrassed, he asked again, and this time the librarian brought him a kid's book about actual stars. He discovered a mind-blowing fact: the sun is a star. In fact, all stars are like the sun, only they are so far away we see them as tiny points of light. Sagan would later say, "The scale of the universe suddenly opened up to me. [It was a] kind of religious experience. [There] was a magnificence to it, a grandeur, a scale which has never left me. Never ever left me."

Another transformative childhood experience was the 1939 World's Fair, which took place in Queens, New York, and was known as "The World of Tomorrow." Sagan was mesmerized by the things of the future like robots and television. But he was also taken with a project that gathered typical American objects in a "time capsule" or container to be buried 50 feet below the earth, not to be opened for 5,000 years (until the year 6939). The capsule contained things like a copy of *Life* magazine, a Mickey Mouse Cup, coins, Camel cigarettes, and seeds for popular crops. They were all things that would show future civilizations about our life on Earth. For the young Sagan, this must have planted the idea that future civilizations we might not be able to imagine today were out there.

Sagan studied astronomy and astrophysics, and his scientific contributions were considerable. He was able to show that Venus's climate is extremely hot (900 degrees Fahrenheit) and not at all similar to Earth's, and that the changing colors of Mars are due to dust storms and not the existence of plant life, as previously thought. But Sagan would also stand outside the scientific community because he was more interested in making science accessible for the general public, and not just for other scientists and science students. He also stood apart in that he believed that other life-forms existed. In other words, he thought that we were not alone.

Then, in 1977, NASA launched two sister spacecrafts that could travel 40,000 miles per hour and were designed to visit Venus, Mars, and Jupiter. There was so much excitement about the potential to connect with other life-forms that Carl Sagan, who never gave up on the idea that extraterrestrial life existed, was called upon to create a message for other life-forms. Updating the idea of the time capsule from the World's Fair that he saw as a child, Sagan created what became known as the Golden Record. It included recordings of waves, wind, thunder, birds, and whales. It has greetings in 55 languages, including some ancient languages. There is

Photo courtesy of NASA/JPL-Caltech

What message would you send to aliens in distant galaxies?

everything from Mozart to Chuck Berry. The record has 116 images of subjects as varied as the double helix, a fetus in the womb, Olympic runners, and a person eating ice cream. Directions for how to play the record were included in hand-drawn symbols etched onto the record. He knew it was highly unlikely that a bunch of aliens would sit around a campfire on Jupiter and listen to Mozart. But he said this, and I think it's the real message of the project: "The launching of this bottle into the cosmic ocean says something very hopeful about life on this planet."

PROJECT # 7
TIME CAPSULE

You'll need:

- Paper and pen or pencil, or a computer
- Envelope
- Objects that reflect who you are (You might include a baseball, a pen, sketches, a dollar, a toy, or a book. You might include a picture of yourself or your family, or even a brief biography of yourself.)
- Shoebox, hat box, or cardboard box of any sort
- Small recording device to record your voice, favorite songs, or other sounds (crickets, birdsongs, your dog barking, etc.) (optional)
- Plastic wrap, foil, and/or a plastic garbage bag
- Heavy-duty duct tape
- Shovel (optional)

1. USING A PAPER AND PEN OR PENCIL, OR BY TYPING ON A COMPUTER, WRITE A LETTER TO THE PERSON/ALIEN WHO WILL FIND THE CAPSULE. TELL THEM WHAT YOU WANT THEM TO KNOW ABOUT YOURSELF AND PLANET EARTH. PUT YOUR LETTER IN AN ENVELOPE, AND ON THE FRONT OF THE ENVELOPE YOU MIGHT ALSO WRITE: "DON'T OPEN UNTIL [PICK A YEAR]."

2. GATHER OBJECTS THAT SAY SOMETHING ABOUT YOU AND LIFE ON EARTH AND PLACE THEM WITH YOUR LETTER INSIDE YOUR BOX.

3. IF YOU'D LIKE, INCLUDE RECORDINGS OF MUSIC, VOICES, AND FAMILIAR SOUNDS.

4. MAKE YOUR CAPSULE AS WATERPROOF AS POSSIBLE USING LAYERS OF PLASTIC WRAP, FOIL, AND GARBAGE BAGS, SEALING IT WITH HEAVY-DUTY DUCT TAPE.

5. FIND A PLACE TO BURY YOUR CAPSULE, JUST PROBABLY NOT YOUR PARENTS' FRONT LAWN. DIG A HOLE DEEP AND WIDE ENOUGH TO HIDE IT COMPLETELY. COVER THE CAPSULE WITH SOIL. AND YOU'RE DONE. THE FUTURE AWAITS. ANOTHER OPTION IS TO HIDE IT IN A CRAWL SPACE IN A HOUSE OR APARTMENT. IT WOULD BE A FUN THING FOR THE NEXT PERSON WHO LIVES IN THE HOUSE TO FIND.

ARE WE THERE YET?

It was the launch of Sputnik that inspired Ed Stone to pursue space physics. After earning his PhD, he became a researcher at the California Institute of Technology (Caltech), famous for its science, engineering, and research programs. As a young professor, he worked part-time at JPL, the Jet Propulsion Laboratory at Caltech, which was becoming one of the leading robotic spacecraft labs in the world. An accidental explosion prompted the program to move to the San Gabriel Mountains. It was eventually taken over by NASA and grew into one of the leading robotic spacecraft labs in the world. This is where Ed Stone would spend a significant part of his career. According to Stone, understanding other planets is crucial to understanding Earth.

Stone was appointed to serve as the chief scientist for the Voyager program (the one that carried the Golden Record). The first mission was to photograph the giant outer planets: Jupiter, Saturn, Uranus, and Neptune. The probes were able to get close enough to one of Jupiter's moons to see active volcanoes there. On another one of Jupiter's moons, the mission found evidence suggesting that there is a liquid water ocean beneath the icy crust. For over thirty years, the Voyagers have been transmitting data from beyond the orbits of our solar system's most distant planets. In 2012, *Voyager* 1 became the first human-made object to reach interstellar space, which means it went outside the "bubble" of magnetic fields and particles created by our sun's solar wind.

There was a time when NASA debated discontinuing the Voyager project, but Stone and a few of his colleagues could not walk away. They managed to secure continued funding and carried on their work from their latest "mission control," based in an office park next to a puppy training center. A homemade cardboard sign near a computer monitor read: "Voyager Mission Critical Hardware—Please do not touch." All that mattered was that they could continue to monitor

Voyager 1 and 2 as the probes eventually reached interstellar space.

In 2019, at age eighty-three, Dr. Stone was still gathering data. That year, he got the recognition he deserved when he was awarded the prestigious Shaw Prize in Astronomy along with a $1.2 million award. His lifelong quest has been to understand our neighborhood in the galaxy. What's out there beyond the earth? And how did it get there? Speaking on *Voyager* 1's momentous feat, Stone said, "We believe this is humankind's historic leap into interstellar space. . . . We can now answer the question we've all been asking—'Are we there yet?' Yes, we are."

Photo courtesy of NASA/JPL–Caltech

Ed Stone standing in front of a life-size model of Voyager.

When the last crewed NASA mission went to the moon, they brought back the first photograph of the earth with its entire visible surface illuminated. It's still one of the most famous photographs of all time. It's called *The Blue Marble*, and every time I see it, I feel the same sense of awe. What is our place in the universe? What responsibility do we have to preserve and protect it? What is the purpose of space travel? What is the mission? When someone asked the British mountain climber George Mallory—who was part of the first three expeditions up Mount Everest—why people attempt to climb the mountain, he gave the famous response, "Because it's there." Are we attempting to go to Mars, as we did the moon, to look for life, to meet Martians, to advance knowledge, for financial gain, or for galactic dominance? Or is the reason simpler than all of that: Because it's there?

I suspect the next time people's minds will be blown in the same way as the moon landing is when someone walks on Mars. This could happen in your lifetime. NASA is developing a program called Artemis, which aims to set up a space station in the moon's orbit and use what we learn there to

Photo courtesy of NASA

The Blue Marble.

reach Mars by 2033. That's not that far away! And billionaires Jeff Bezos (the founder of Amazon) and Elon Musk (the founder of the Tesla car company and SpaceX, the first private company to send humans to the International Space Station.) are also dedicating funds and resources to reach Mars. As long as there is space, people will race to explore it. I think Stephen Hawking said it best when he said, "We explore because we are human, and we want to know."

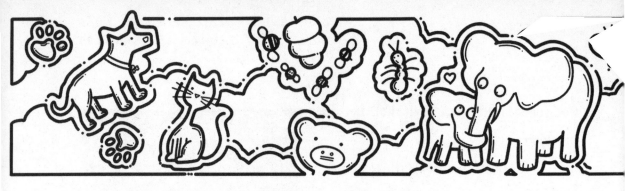

ANIMAL BEHAVIOR

CHAPTER SIX

I call it checking pee-mail. It's when your dog stops to sniff every plant, tree trunk, and fire hydrant—pretty much everything you find on an average walk. Most dog owners tend to yank their dog away when they take too long sniffing. The thing is, your dog *needs* to sniff around to find out what's going on in its world. Your dog learns a whole lot from sniffing other dogs' pee, most importantly what other dogs have been there and when, depending on how fresh the pee is. And when they pee in the same spot, it's called scent marking and it's extremely important to them; it's part of how they communicate. Tracking the comings and goings of other dogs is a way of keeping in touch, like how people who work in offices will congregate around a water cooler to talk about the weather, sports, and what's on TV. Dogs and humans have one major thing in common: We're social animals. We like to know what's going on with each other.

Dogs and humans go way back. Just as we evolved from primates, dogs evolved from wolves. Dogs were the first animals to live with humans. We call this domestication, which describes how an animal goes from being in the wild to becoming our furry friend who watches Netflix beside us on the couch. Scientists agree that all dogs descended from wolves, but there is still debate over when, where, and exactly how this happened. The when is between 15,000 and 40,000 years ago. The where is either in East Asia or Europe, or both. Scientists studying doggie DNA from all over the world, through extensive sampling of teeth and bone fossils, are becoming more convinced that the process of domestication may have started in both parts of the world. The more fascinating question to me is how. Or, as Brian Handwerk in *Smithsonian Magazine* puts it, "How did dogs go from being our bitter rivals to our snuggly, fluffy pooch pals?"

Here, too, scientists have different theories. Some scientists believe that dog domestication occurred when early humans were hunter-gatherers who hunted in packs, and that hunting with wolves made both the humans and the wolves more successful at killing prey. According to this theory, wolves began to scavenge the waste and scraps of human communities and became acculturated or used to living near humans. Animals also became easier to domesticate as they lost their fear of people. For their part, humans began to see how useful wolves could be in helping to hunt, and in protecting homes and families. Once wolves started feeding on human scraps and grew more comfortable around humans, the whole relationship began to evolve.

Others dispute this idea, claiming that wolves, as predators, were much more successful hunters than humans, given their speed, sharp teeth, and keen sense of smell. Then again, human hunters were making stone tools and weapons that aided in the killing of large animals. Another theory is that when humans first began to farm and form settlements, they adopted wolf pups and raised them into domestication. The theory that turns out to be right will be largely dependent on whether or not wolves were domesticated before the invention of agriculture or after people started farming. New research with genomic sequencing of ancient DNA suggests that wolves started turning into dogs before agriculture started.

As wolves began to shed some of their predatory behaviors, they became humans' protectors and helpers, eventually herding sheep, guarding families from other predators, and pulling sleds. Decoration on murals and on pottery from ancient Egypt, Greece, Rome, and China depicts dogs wearing collars, indicating they had by that time already become pets. You would not be able to get a collar and leash on a wolf living in the wild!

Though people first started breeding dogs for different uses thousands of years ago, things really took off in nineteenth-century England, which is when a large portion of the dog breeds we know today were created. Hunting dogs were bred for tracking different kinds of animals. Larger dogs, like standard poodles, were used for hunting bears. Farmers relied on working breeds, such as collies and sheepdogs, to help them guard and herd sheep. Terriers were used for hunting smaller critters, like badgers and rats. And the fastest dog, the greyhound, hunted rabbits. Dogs were also bred as companions, especially for the aristocracy who favored "cute" dogs or "lap" dogs, such as Pomeranians and pugs. The reason dogs are easy to train is because they *want* to please; they enjoy petting and praise. They have become social animals and

Believe it or not, these two are related.

are hyper-friendly. Today, there are over 300 breeds of dogs.

Even after thousands of years of evolution, a dog's paw and a wolf's paw still have the same basic shape, so much so that you can't really tell them apart. In the winters when my sister and I were young, we would find animal prints in the snow, not just from dogs, but from deer and rabbits as well, and sometimes we'd follow them to see where they led. In the spring, we'd sometimes come across tracks from squirrels, birds, and cats in the mud. We used our encyclopedia to identify which footprint belonged to which animal. Now you can easily find this information on the internet.

PROJECT #1
PAW PRINTS (DOMESTIC)

You'll need:

- Newspaper
- Measuring cups
- 4 cups plaster of paris (Do not use old plaster of paris. It won't set up properly and will crack.)
- 2 cups cold tap water
- 7-cup plastic container
- Mixing spoon
- Disposable aluminum cake pan, about 9" x 9" x 1 ½"
- Spatula
- Dog, cat, or any other animal

INSTRUCTIONS

1.

SPREAD OUT NEWSPAPER ON YOUR WORK SURFACE.

2. PLACE PLASTER OF PARIS AND WATER IN A PLASTIC CONTAINER. USE YOUR MIXING SPOON TO STIR WELL UNTIL YOUR MIXTURE IS THE CONSISTENCY OF PANCAKE BATTER.

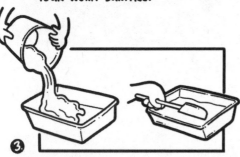

3. POUR THE MIXTURE INTO THE ALUMINUM CAKE PAN AND SMOOTH IT WITH A SPATULA. LET IT REST FOR AN HOUR TO SET.

4.

PLACE YOUR DOG'S PAW (OR THE PAW/FOOT OF ANY OTHER ANIMAL) ONTO THE MIXTURE AND PRESS IT DOWN ABOUT ½ TO ¾ INCH – PRESS FIRMLY. YOUR DOG WILL PROBABLY BE MORE COOPERATIVE IF YOU SET THE PLASTER OF PARIS CONTAINER ON THE TABLE AND THE DOG ON YOUR LAP.

6. ALLOW THE PLASTE OF PARIS TO DRY FOR 24 HOURS, AND YOU'LL HAVE A LIFE-SIZE KEEPSAKE OF YOUR PETS PAW.

5.  REMOVE YOUR DOG'S PAW AND RINSE THOROUGHLY.

NOTE: IF YOU DON'T HAVE ANY DOMESTIC OR OUTDOOR ANIMALS, YOU CAN ALWAYS USE A HUMAN "PAW."

———— PAW PRINTS (WILD) ————

If you are lucky enough to find an animal print in the mud, you can also make a cast of it where you find it. You will need the same materials, plus:

- Dirt
- Roll of paper towels

INSTRUCTIONS

1. CLEAN THE AREA AROUND THE PAW PRINT YOU DISCOVERED, REMOVING TWIGS, LEAVES, OR OTHER DEBRIS SO YOU CAN OBTAIN A CLEAN CAST.

2. MAKE A CIRCLE AROUND THE PRINT WITH A MOUND OF DIRT.

3. CAREFULLY POUR THE PLASTER OF PARIS INTO THE PRINT, FILLING IT UP SLIGHTLY OVER THE TOP OF THE PRINT. SMOOTH THE SURFACE WITH YOUR SPATULA.

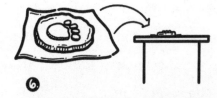

4. ALLOW THE PLASTER OF PARIS TO SET FOR AN HOUR.

5. WHEN IT IS SOMEWHAT FIRM TO THE TOUCH, DIG AROUND THE PERIMETER OF THE CAST TO GENTLY PRY IT UP FROM THE GROUND.

6. PLACE YOUR PRINT ON PAPER TOWELS ON A FLAT SURFACE TO DRY OVERNIGHT.

I never planned on becoming an animal scientist, though looking back I see that there were signs all along the way. The first came in the form of Tucky and Hunter, two neighborhood dogs that basically stayed outside all day (dogs pretty much don't get to do that anymore due to leash laws, which is sad because dogs like roaming, patrolling, and interacting with each other and people). But the difference between these two dogs was marked. Tucky loved to chase tennis balls. He was a skinny, frisky guy, and he couldn't get enough of fetching them. He would jump over fences to retrieve a ball. When you were tired of playing, he would drop the ball at your feet and look at you with his big eyes until you picked up the ball and threw it again. Hunter couldn't care less about chasing anything. He was heavyset and content to sit under the shade of a tree and watch the world go by. What accounted for this difference? I didn't know, but I was interested in how two dogs could be so unalike.

The next sign came when I went away to boarding school. I had gotten kicked out of my high school for throwing a heavy book at the head of a girl who called me a retard. As a result, my mother had to find a new school for me, and she chose one that had a riding program. Today, it is documented that riding horses can have a therapeutic effect on people with autism. Through my relationship with horses, I learned more self-control, to focus better, and to connect. My feelings still get hurt when someone teases me, but I no longer throw books at them.

When I was fourteen years old, I was put in charge of the stables at the school, including feeding and grooming the horses, mucking out the stalls, riding, and showing the horses. I kept the saddles and tack clean and orderly. I even reroofed the barn. None of these things ever felt like chores to me. It was a way of respecting the animals I loved. Some kids at school didn't respect the animals and treated them poorly. I knew it was wrong and I was really upset about it, but I didn't want to tattle. I would do anything not to risk my job in the barn. It was also the only place where I was never bullied. I wanted to keep it that way.

For me, riding was a kind of freedom I hadn't experienced before.

Galloping most of all was extremely exciting. It was like flying. Since I couldn't tolerate hugging or other physical contact, riding gave me a physical connection. Every move you make with a horse, from riding in a saddle to making a clicking sound to pulling back on the reins or patting the horse's neck or letting him eat a carrot from your hand, is a meaningful connection.

Visiting my aunt's ranch in Arizona started me on a career path in the livestock industry.

As with Tucky and Hunter, I came to know two horses whose behavior couldn't be more different. Goldie (named for her hay-colored coat) was great in the ring but went crazy on the trail. I later learned that Goldie had been abused before she came to my school. The owner of the school bought horses inexpensively at horse auctions, and some of them had been abused or abandoned. As a result, they came with a host of behavioral problems, such as biting, rearing up, and refusing to leave the stall. King, a large grade horse (meaning we don't know his parents or what kind of horse he is) was well behaved in the ring and on the trails, but when you took him to a horse show, he went wild, rearing up and trying to bolt. I suspected it was due to all kinds of new stimuli, such as balloons, big crowds of people, and being petted by strangers. I knew instinctively that animals need to be gradually introduced to new things.

I figured this out because it was also true of me. Because of my autism, I had drastic responses to stimuli like loud noises, being held, and scratchy clothes. Any sudden loud sound or scratchy new fabric and I would end up in a meltdown. Eventually, I put it together. Some horses had the same reactions to things as I did, such as a scratchy pad under a saddle, or sudden noises like a car backfiring, or people getting too close too quickly. Because I understood what the animals were going through, I believed that animals had emotions and they were similar to mine.

When I went to graduate school to study animal behavior, everything I believed to be true was turned upside down. A famous psychologist and theorist named B. F. Skinner believed that all behavior is based on something called conditioning. This means that behavior is based on a system of rewards and punishments. If someone gets praise from their parents after doing well on a test, they are more likely to try to do well on tests in the future. Or if someone is grounded for not doing chores, they are less likely to skip chores in the future. Skinner believed that all animal behavior could be explained by rewards and punishments. And it seemed like everyone believed that, too.

OUTSIDE THE BOX

Growing up in Susquehanna, Pennsylvania, in the early 1900s, Frederic Skinner and his younger brother liked to explore their yard and the woods and river beyond their house. All his games seemed to involve some kind of scientific experimentation. Fred would catch bees in hollyhock blossoms and bring cocoons inside to watch the butterflies emerge. More ambitiously, he used a cage-like mousetrap to catch chipmunks that he intended to tame, only to be disappointed when the chipmunks proved

When I was in college, I visited Skinner's actual pigeon lab that you see in this picture.

resistant to domestication. Like many budding scientists, young Skinner preferred building toys to playing with them. He made buildings out of Erector Sets, used the wheels on an abandoned roller skate to make a scooter, and crafted a steerable wagon from the wheels and axles of an old baby carriage.

In college, Skinner studied psychology. But psychology was no longer just the study of the human mind; now people were studying animal behavior as a way to understand humans. Skinner was interested in creating a device that would measure animal behavior. Before Skinner, observing rats in mazes and similar experiments were popular means of studying animal behavior, but they gave highly unreliable results. Remember the boy who tried to tame chipmunks in cages? As an adult, Skinner built a box for experiments that came to be known as a "Skinner box."

The essence of a Skinner box is that an animal can perform a task to receive a reward, usually in the form of food, allowing scientists to take highly precise measurements of the animal's behavior. In one variation of a Skinner box, rats learned to press a lever to get the reward of a food pellet. Another experiment included pigeons pecking a key for food. A Skinner box was able to record the frequency of responses with tremendous accuracy. This process of changing behavior by giving rewards and punishments is called operant conditioning. Skinner concluded that all behavior and emotion were based on a series of rewards and punishments, and his ideas dominated the field of animal studies and human behavior for a long time, though I never quite believed it. Others also disagree with Skinner. Keller Breland and Marian Breland wrote a classic paper in 1961 showing that innate natural behavior patterns also have an effect of animal behavior. They are not academic scientists, so it took longer for their work to be appreciated.

Today, new studies are being done on solitary mammals to see what they might have in common with autistic people. Solitary animals are those that don't live in packs and who lead unsocial lives, like polar bears, skunks, and tigers. Researchers are just beginning to see various biochemical and genetic differences between social and nonsocial animals, such as levels of brain activity and hormones. If we can unlock these mysteries of the brain, we might be able to help people with autism who, like me, have trouble bonding, communicating, making eye contact, and feeling comfortable in social situations.

My intuition told me that animals were capable of thought, memory, and emotions. I believe that Skinner made some very important contributions to animal science, but I also think that observing the way things happen in ordinary life is just as important as testing in a lab, especially when it comes to animals. Experiments only measure what you want to measure. If you are a patient observer, you will discover a great deal about animals without caging them.

One of my first assignments in graduate school was to choose an animal and observe it for four hours. When an animal scientist studies an animal, they use something called an ethogram. An ethogram is a catalog of all observable animal behaviors: the behavior itself, a definition of the behavior, and the frequency with which a behavior occurs. I decided to go to the zoo and observe antelope for my ethogram. I parked myself in one place and wrote down all the behaviors I observed: sleeping, resting, pooping, peeing, and walking around, which they did with some frequency. The shocker came a few hours in when I saw two males in adjacent pens lock horns through a chain-link fence.

This aggressive behavior is a move for dominance. Antelope fight by locking horns. Even though they were kept apart and no longer lived in the wild, their instinct to fight persisted. Had I only observed the antelope for an hour or two, I would have missed this incredible display of competition. That's why time and patience are key.

The observations I had made in Arizona feedlots largely contributed to my becoming an animal scientist and developing safer cattle-handling systems. I was able to see reflections on shiny metal or other visual distractions that made a cow afraid or unwilling to enter a chute. Handlers who had worked in the yards for years didn't see them. The difference: observing. While the handlers were simply trying to do their jobs, I made close, careful observations of how the animals reacted and behaved when they saw a small object moving, such as a dangling chain. Sometimes I got on the ground or in the chute so I could see and feel exactly what the animals were thinking and feeling. The ranchers thought I was nuts, but I figured it out by looking at the world through animal eyes.

It's important to take the animal's habitat into account when learning their behavior. Does your dog live on a farm where it gets to roam free for large parts of the day, interacting with horses, cattle, and cowhands? Or does this dog live in a small apartment and get walked twice a day on a city street to do its business? These differences will affect the dog's behavior. When a person asks me why their dog hides in the closet or rips up all the furniture, the first thing I want to know is: How much time does the dog spend alone, and does the dog live in a small apartment? It's not that hard to figure out. Dogs are intensely social, and when left alone all day, they get lonely.

Being alone will make some dogs sluggish and sleep all day, while others will constantly look out the window or go nuts and tear up the apartment out of anxiety. Some dogs are content in a small space and others suffer from doggie claustrophobia. When you observe behaviors and describe them, you can begin to hypothesize about why a dog does something. The scientific process: observe, hypothesize, test.

Ideally, you could set up a video camera or a "nanny cam" to watch the dog when you're not home. What does it do when no one is interacting with it? When you are home and someone comes to the door or walks by the house, most dogs will bark. Does it bark if you're not home? Also, what is the bark like? Is the dog growling in its throat like a car idling? Is it a nonstop, ferocious bark? Or is the dog just yapping a friendly hello? In my neighborhood, the condos are closely grouped, and when I take a walk in the afternoon when the occupants are not at home, I can hear dogs whining and barking. There is no dog park nearby, and I think the dogs are hungry for social life. I've worked with my colleagues and students on studies that show dogs left home alone for too long turn gray prematurely. They are like prisoners in solitary confinement. Dogs in shelters need people to play with them so they can build trust in humans and successfully transition into living with a family. Too often the problem is we've bred and raised dogs to be our friends, only to not make time to play with them. To give a dog a good life in a town with strict leash laws requires a lot of effort to provide the dogs with a social life with both people and other dogs.

Full and accurate findings require the scientist to observe an animal all times of the day, especially if they are observing in the wild. An ethogram tracks the way behavior changes depending on the time of day and builds a profile for an animal's daily routine. You are looking for cyclical behavior, or in other words, things the animal reliably does at the same time every day. In this way, you learn its habits, patterns, and behaviors.

From there you can both predict behavior and interpret it. What does it mean that my cat sleeps on the back of the couch every day from 3:00 to 5:00 p.m.? Why does my dog wolf down its breakfast but pick at its dinner? Why does my dog growl only at men? Why do some animals, especially in zoos, pace back and forth? This behavior is called stereotypies and signals distress in the animal. As with people, we need to learn how the animals got anxious and depressed in order to help them. All these questions can be answered via close observation over time.

PROJECT #2
ETHOGRAM

You'll need:
- Notebook
- Pencil
- Patience

INSTRUCTIONS

AGE: 3
WEIGHT: 45 lbs.
SEX: FEMALE
NATURAL HABITAT: HOUSE

LIST OF BEHAVIORS	DATE	FREQUENCY	NOTES
SLEEPING AND/OR NAPPING	6/3	TWICE	8am & 3pm
EATING	EVERYDAY	TWICE	7:30am & 6pm
MOUTH LICKING	6/10	ONCE	WHEN SHE SAW MOM GET THE ICE CREAM OUT OF THE FREEZER!
DRINKING			
PLAYING WITH OTHER DOGS			
TAIL WAGGING			
NUZZLING HUMANS	6/15	ALL DAY	WHEN COUSIN VINNIE VISITED.
SHOWING BELLY	6/23	ONCE	WHEN DAD CAME HOME AFTER WORK
GROWLING			
BITING			
FIGHTING WITH OTHER DOGS			
SEEKING PETTING/PLAYING	6/8	ONCE	AFTER SCHOOL SHE BROUGHT ME HER FAVORITE CHEW TOY!
SHOWING ALERT POSTURE WHEN HEARING NOISE	MON.-FRI.		EVERYTIME THE BIG BROWN DELIVERY TRUCK
BARKING			
WHAT DOG EXPLORES AND SMELLS ON A WALK			
PEEING & POOPING (Scientifically known as urination and defecation)	EVERYDAY	TWICE	SHE POOPS AND PEES WHEN MOM LETS HER OUT IN THE MORNINGS AND NIGHTS. THE POOPS SMELL REALLY BAD. AND DAD SAYS FUNNY THINGS WHEN HE STEPS IN AN OLD POOP!
GROOMING ITSELF			
OTHER			

The author Elizabeth Marshall Thomas took the idea of an ethogram one step further. She posed a question that few, if any, before had attempted to answer: What do dogs do when left on their own? Most studies of dogs focused on what their behavior could tell us about human behavior. Thomas didn't care about that. For almost two years, she followed a dog she sometimes watched for a friend. Like a detective, she "trailed" Misha, a husky who loved to slip out at night. Normally, a dog disappearing into the night is cause for worry, but Misha always came home unharmed. Thomas decided to see where he was going and what he was up to. What she learned was how Misha navigated the busy streets of Boston, how he avoided getting hit by cars, where he scavenged for food, and where he chose to leave his scent (pee).

Elizabeth Marshall Thomas doesn't draw many conclusions about dogs as a species other than that they prefer to be with each other rather than with humans. She found that Misha roamed around approximately 130 square miles, which is similar to the 200- to 500-square-mile range of wolves. She concluded that the purpose of his adventures was to be around other dogs. She wanted to understand dogs on their own terms and did so just by observing them from a distance.

I've always admired scientists who do their work in "the field." It was Jane Goodall who first inspired me to see the world through an animal's eyes and in the context of their habitat. She went to the African bush to observe chimpanzees and dedicated the rest of her life to understanding them and saving them from extinction. Some scientists didn't agree with her methods, believing that scientists need to remain "objective" at all times, meaning they shouldn't form emotional bonds with their subjects. For Goodall, her years of observation yielded original research and also showed the close bond humans share with our closest relative.

NOT SO PLAIN JANE

Do you believe in destiny? In 1935, when Jane Goodall was a little over one year old, her father gave her a stuffed toy chimpanzee. He was named Jubilee to commemorate the first chimp born at the London Zoo. Jane would become world famous for her work with chimpanzees in Africa. There is a family story that a young Jane collected earthworms and brought them into bed with her, until her mother explained they wouldn't be able to live away from the dirt. She loved making secret places in the garden, watching birds make nests and spiders carry egg sacs. Her dog, Rusty, was a constant companion as Jane roamed the cliffs watching weasels hunt mice, hedgehogs pursue mates, and squirrels bury beechnuts. She was especially entertained watching blue jays steal the nuts.

The most revealing story about the young girl destined to become a scientist involves a chicken and an egg. Jane knew that chickens come from eggs, but she couldn't imagine where the eggs came out of the hen. Remember, YouTube wasn't an option back then. She crawled into the henhouse and waited to see firsthand a chicken lay an egg. It took four hours, but she got what she was looking for. Satisfied, she returned to her house, where her parents had been frantically looking for her. They had even called the police!

For all her love of nature, Jane Goodall found her calling by reading books. She loved every Tarzan book, and within those pages her dream of going to Africa was born. Jane was studying to become a secretary when an old friend called with an offer. Her family had just bought a farm in Kenya; would Jane like to visit? Jane later wrote, "I could go to Africa—and my life would be changed forever."

In Africa, Jane met world-famous paleontologist Louis Leakey and became his personal secretary. She was fascinated by his work, including the proposition that the great ape was man's closest living relative. When he suggested that she do some fieldwork observing chimpanzees in the Gombe Stream National Park in Tanzania, she felt underqualified. All she had was a two-year secretarial degree. Plus, there were no established guidelines for how to observe chimpanzees. They were dangerous animals, at least four times stronger than humans, but she jumped at the chance to observe the chimps up close and personal.

Goodall's first attempt to get close to the chimps failed. She realized she had to visit them at the same time every day and give them their space. It took two years, but she eventually earned their trust, sharing bananas with them. Goodall wrote, "I already felt that I belonged to this new forest world, that this was where I was meant to be." Goodall made at least three breakthroughs observing chimpanzees. First, it was assumed that chimps were vegetarians, but it turns out they are omnivores like us, meaning they eat both meat and veggies. Second, Jane found they both make and use tools (again like us), and third, they have highly developed social behaviors. They kiss, snuggle, and pat each other on the back. They can also be aggressive, fighting and throwing dirt at each other. She also observed how chimpanzees organize themselves in hierarchies and take care of the community. Though some people felt she broke all scientific rules of objective observation by getting close to the chimps, giving them names instead of numbers, I believe her fifty years of fieldwork into chimpanzee behavior is a monumental contribution to our understanding of animals and ourselves.

Michel Gunther/Science Source

Jane Goodall's work in the field with chimps has changed the way we see ourselves.

PROJECT #3
STUFFED TOY CHIMPANZEE

Tip: *Find a picture of a chimpanzee on the internet or in a book for reference.*

You'll need:

- Pencil
- Tracing paper
- Black cotton cloth (though you could substitute with any cloth)
- Pins
- Scissors
- Needle and thread
- Stuffing
- Brown, black, and tan felt
- Glue gun or regular glue
- Cardboard
- Clear nail polish

INSTRUCTIONS

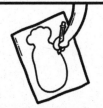

1. USE YOUR PENCIL TO TRACE THE SHAPE OF A CHIMPANZEE (JUST THE BODY AND HEAD) ON TRACING PAPER.

2. FOLD YOUR CLOTH IN HALF AND PIN YOUR TRACING PAPER TO IT.

3. CUT AROUND THE LINES.

4. SEW 3/4 OF THE WAY AROUND THE TWO PIECES OF CLOTH.

5. FILL THE CAVITY WITH STUFFING AND SEW UP THE REST.

6. REPEAT STEPS 1 THROUGH 5 FOR THE TWO ARMS AND LEGS.

7. SEW THE LIMBS ONTO THE BODY.

8. CUT OUT BROWN FELT DOTS FOR EYES AND A NOSE. CUT A CIRCLE OF TAN FELT FOR THE AREA AROUND THE MOUTH AND TWO BLACK STRIPS FOR THE LIPS. USE A GLUE GUN OR REGULAR GLUE TO ATTACH.

9. CUT OUT CARDBOARD FINGERNAILS AND APPLY MANY COATS OF POLISH TO MAKE THEM CLAWLIKE. ATTACH THEM WITH A GLUE GUN.

DO YOU FEEL ME?

Frans de Waal started collecting small animals at a young age. He grew up in the Netherlands in the 1950s and collected everything from salamanders and frogs to mice and birds. When he went to university to study animal science, there was one problem: academics only worked with dead animals. This was not what he had in mind. But there was another problem as well. The field was still dominated by followers of B. F. Skinner. Not only did Skinner believe that animals had no emotion, he also concluded that while animals could learn, they could not think in the way that humans can. De Waal set out on a six-year study of chimpanzees at the Royal Burgers' Zoo. What he observed would help change the way we think of animals and ourselves in relation to them.

De Waal observed the chimps exhibiting facial expressions that mirrored our own. And they also expressed qualities such as empathy and altruism, putting others first. Again, very human qualities. Even more profound was that these qualities are the basis of moral behavior, which is a product of our ability to understand right and wrong. Ask any animal owner if their pets have emotions and they will rattle off stories that display a range of emotions. De Waal believed that when we talk about animals as the sum of their physical responses, which was the Skinner approach, we miss the important emotional connection.

For instance, rats will flatten their ears and narrow their eyes when in anguish. Elephants use their trunks to console each other. The title of de Waal's book *Mama's Last Hug* comes from the story of the chimpanzee Mama who, nearing the end of her life, greeted a scientist whom she had known for over forty years with a big smile while she embraced him and patted him on the neck, a very human gesture shared by many primates as well.

De Waal also pointed out that scientific animal studies were virtually all conducted in laboratories. Observing chimps in a setting much closer to their natural habitat, he saw that they were capable of problem-solving, facial recognition, and showing a range of emotions through heavy or quick breathing, sweating, noises, and expressive body language. De Waal was able to distinguish between emotion and feeling. Emotions are what we can see on the surface, he noted, while feelings are what lie beneath the surface and can vary greatly. Humans can tell us about their feelings, but animals (at least so far) can only show us their emotions.

My brain works differently from most people's, and for a long time all people could see was what I couldn't do. I struggled with speech, with connecting to people, with making eye contact, and I repeated phrases and sentences in a loop. It was only when I put all the pieces together and saw how my brain more closely aligned with how animals think and respond that I was able not only to make contributions to animal science but also to better understand myself.

I first realized this ability going all the way back to my aunt's ranch and being able to pick out the things that frightened the cattle. I've said this before: *animals perceive things humans can't perceive.* If you have any doubt about the unique way animals perceive things, think about all the ways we use dogs to assist us: seeing-eye dogs for the blind, dogs who assist mentally and physically disabled people, military dogs who sniff out bombs, police dogs who help find missing people, therapy dogs; I've even read about dogs who are able to detect cancer. It's also true that some animals can remember highly detailed information we can't remember. Dogs, for instance, have 300 million sensory receptors for smell compared with humans, who have a mere six million, which is why you want a dog to look for you if you get lost. Dogs, with their amazing sense of smell, have tracked people who are lost in the wilderness, who have been trapped by debris from earthquakes or avalanches. They smell odors that are undetectable to humans.

When I work with my students on developing projects to understand animal behavior, we want to understand the world through their eyes and senses. We want to understand the animal on its own terms. For example, we were recently interested in testing horse perception. I worked with my student Megan Corgan to set up a child's outdoor plastic play set with a slide and walked the horse by it a few times. The first couple of times we walked the horse by the play set, he stopped and didn't want to pass by it. Eventually, he was able to pass the play set as if it had always been there.

Then we turned the set around. We wanted to observe the horse's reaction. Approaching the play set from this new angle completely confused the horse. It was as if he had never seen it before, and once again he wouldn't walk past. To us, a play set is a play set no matter what angle we come at it. This is, in part, because we think in words. We know what a play set is and can imagine different kinds, no problem. But a horse thinks in pictures. Every new play set, or even the same play set at a different angle, will need to be examined all over again. Once you get away from language-based thought, you can more easily imagine how animals think and better understand their behavior. The scientist E. O. Wilson cracked the code with ants when he realized that they used sensory-based perceptions to do all the remarkable things they do.

THE ANTS GO MARCHING ONE BY ONE

As a boy in the 1930s, Edward O. Wilson came across a jellyfish threaded with red lines on the shore of Paradise Beach, Florida. He watched it until dusk and went back the next morning, but it was gone. It was a memory he recalled decades later in his memoir. He spent his days searching for treasure up and down the shoreline, only taking breaks for lunch and dinner. He dreamed of finding monsters and giants of the deep, and what he found only expanded his imagination: stingrays, blue crabs, sea trout, toadfish, and a pod of bottlenose porpoises. "It was the animals of that place that cast a lasting spell," he wrote.

Then something happened that would alter the course of his life. One day when he was fishing, he caught a pinfish, and as he jerked it out of the water, it flung up into his face. The sharp spines on the fish's back punctured the pupil in his right eye. The incident left Wilson completely blinded in that eye. With his vision deeply compromised, he turned his attention to the world of ants and insects. Luckily, Wilson's left eye could see things up close and in great detail. He said he could see the "hairs on the bodies of small insects." Wilson started collecting harvester ants in sand-filled jars, which he kept under his bed. It's hard to imagine his mother's reaction when she vacuumed his room, but Wilson was certain of his destiny. He knew then that he would become an entomologist, a person who studies and specializes in insects.

His family moved to Washington, D.C., in close proximity to the

National Museum of Natural History. While some kids might spend all their time looking at a *T. rex* skeleton, Wilson pored over trays of butterflies and insects. He made a homemade butterfly net with a broomstick, coat hanger, and cheesecloth bags. Then a fifth-grade teacher complimented his writing abilities and knowledge of insects. "The course of my life had been set," he later said.

At sixteen, he decided to become a world authority on ants and started collecting species in small bottles filled with alcohol. Using the classic field guide on ants, he compared the ants with those in the book to make positive identifications. He also took notes on the ants' habits and nests. Wilson recalled finding a huge colony of ants under the bark of a rotting tree, which opened a window into a whole new subterranean world.

Many years later, Wilson's experiments with ants would prove that communication exists among animals that we had never known. Finding and identifying species was only the beginning. Wilson went on to unlock some of the greatest mysteries about ants and insect behavior. The secret to ant communication is smell. If you've ever wondered why ants seem to move in single-file lines, it's because they leave odor trails. Wilson was able to determine that taste and smell, not sight and sound, are essential to ant communication. And in learning about communication, Wilson also helped pioneer the field of sociobiology, which studies how biological factors influence social behavior in animals. "I was seven years old," he wrote, "and every species, large and small, was a wonder to be examined, thought about, and, if possible, captured and examined again."

SIGHTING MONARCH BUTTERFLIES

You can be part of a worldwide effort to keep track of butterflies as they migrate across the country, helping scientists collect much-needed data about their numbers, which corresponds to all sorts of important scientific data about climate change, pollination, food supply, etc. If you report all these, it will help scientists track monarch populations, which in turn provides information on the ecosystem and our environment. Check out this website if you want to share your information with other citizen scientists; there are easy forms to send in your data: journeynorth.org /monarchs. Or you can just keep track of butterflies in your area.

You'll need:

- Pencil
- Map of your state
- Tracing paper
- Bulletin board (optional)

- Tape (optional)
- Marker or pushpins
- Notebook or poster board

INSTRUCTIONS

1. TRACE YOUR STATE ONTO A PIECE OF PAPER. NOTE THE MAJOR CITIES AND RIVERS. PUT IT ON A BULLETIN BOARD OR TAPE IT TO YOUR WALL. THIS WILL BE A VISUAL RECORD OF WHERE YOU SPOT BUTTERFLIES.

2. WHEN YOU SPOT A MONARCH EITHER PUT A PUSHPIN ON THE MAP OR MAKE A DOT WITH A MARKER.

(CONTINUED)

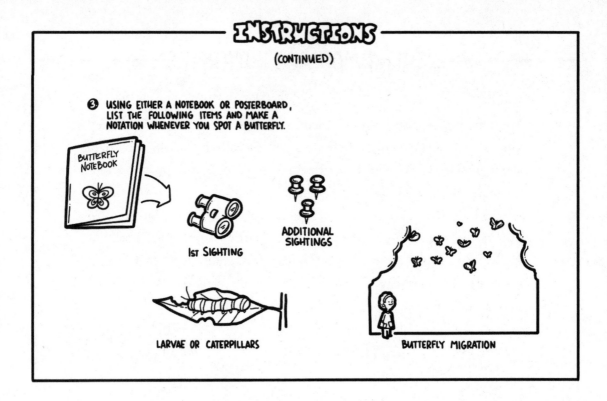

❸ USING EITHER A NOTEBOOK OR POSTERBOARD, LIST THE FOLLOWING ITEMS AND MAKE A NOTATION WHENEVER YOU SPOT A BUTTERFLY.

BUTTERFLY NOTEBOOK

1st SIGHTING

ADDITIONAL SIGHTINGS

LARVAE OR CATERPILLARS

BUTTERFLY MIGRATION

Seventy percent of students I teach in the animal studies department at Colorado State University want to become veterinarians. I've discovered that most of the students don't know about any other careers that involve animals. Many of our students, once exposed to other fields, have found satisfying careers in research, genetics, breeding, nutrition, and training search-and-rescue and seeing-eye dogs. Some students become involved in animal welfare, making sure animals are treated humanely. And some extend that mission globally as they pursue the field of wildlife management and saving endangered animals.

I work with students who devise experiments to understand different aspects of animal behavior. One of my students, Christa Coppola, found that dogs kept in animal shelters will be less stressed if a volunteer comes in every day and takes them for walks and plays with them. In another experiment, it was discovered that cattle that became agitated during handling had lower weight gain. Performing veterinary procedures on zoo animals is stressful unless the animals have been trained to voluntarily cooperate. Research performed in our research group showed that even flighty animals, such as antelope, can be trained to cooperate with having injections if they get treats.

I'm not interested in how many times a rat can press a lever. Setting up experiments like that only tells us how animals respond under laboratory conditions and according to how humans see the world. Understanding animals is best accomplished by observing through their eyes in their habitat. I recently learned about the work of Jill Pruetz, who has a lot in common with Jane Goodall. She studies chimps in the savannas of Senegal, where she made the remarkable observations that chimps were using tools to hunt and were sharing food, things we thought only humans did. This is huge. This connects us even more to our closest relative than we thought.

Pruetz tells a remarkable story of a day when a group of chimpanzees were scared off by hunters and left a nine-month-old behind. Pruetz raced to the site, cared for the chimp's wounds, and slept beside her. Returning the baby to its mother took great care. "We put her in a sack when we got close to the chimps because we wanted to leave her and move away so the chimps wouldn't see us with the baby—we were afraid they would attack us upon seeing we had the baby." It reminded me of those little blue eggs in the nest outside our living room window, and our mother warning us not to go near them for fear the mother bird would see us as predators.

But when Pruetz and her team left the sack in the designated spot, the baby chimp, confused, didn't call out for her family, and Jill and her team had to bring her even closer, to about 30 feet from where the chimps were feeding in a fig tree. They set the sack down and opened it before moving away. One of the teenage chimps came down to investigate. The baby chimp looked at the chimp and back at Pruetz and her team. Then the teenager smelled her, picked her up, and took her to the tree, where she was reunited with her mother. Pruetz writes, "I followed them for the rest of the day and baby seemed to do fine. She was nursing and even played a little with her mother. She didn't move more than an arm's length from Tia [her mother] for most of the day—and she had one hand on her at all times!"

The way we treat animals reflects our humanity. Returning one baby chimp to its mother may seem like a small thing, but to my mind it's a symbol of the best we can be. We share the planet with animals. It's the least we can do.

Nine-month-old baby chimp Tia just before being reunited with her mom and family.

Courtesy of Dr. Jill Pruetz

CONCLUSION

I n 2019, a sixteen-year-old girl caught my attention and that of the entire world. She started her journey standing alone outside parliament in her hometown of Stockholm with a poster that read "School Strike for Climate." Her name is Greta Thunberg, and from the time she first learned about the damaging effects of climate change to the planet, she devoted herself to climate activism. Her solitary protest resulted in a worldwide strike of 1.6 million people in 133 countries protesting climate change.

Greta Thunberg started learning about climate change when she was eleven years old. It was impossible not to be impressed by this fearless young girl as she addressed the UN Climate Change Conference and a World Economic Forum. She didn't care about her newfound fame or all the attention. She has a single-minded goal: reverse climate change. People also noticed something different about Greta: she spoke in a monotone way, she didn't make much eye contact, and she would not be distracted from her message. Her focus and intensity cut through all the noise.

Greta Thunberg is on the autism spectrum. She has a milder form of

Wikimedia Commons/Anders Hellberg

SKOLSTREJK
FÖR
KLIMATET

Greta Thunberg protesting for climate-change awareness, igniting a new generation of people who care about the environment.

autism than me known as Asperger's syndrome. One of the things she attributes to her success as an activist is her Asperger's. She says she sees the world in black-and-white terms. For her, there is no compromise. She says, "There are no gray areas when it comes to survival." She also says about her condition, "To be different is not a weakness. It's a strength in many ways, because you stand out from the crowd."

There is overwhelming scientific evidence that there are problems in our environment. If we look at just one aspect of life in the natural world, we can see how climate change is affecting the world around us. Take insects. They are responsible for pollinating one-third of our food crop. Over the last twenty-seven years, flying insects have declined 75 percent. Monarch butterflies have decreased by 90 percent in the last twenty years. And bumblebees have fallen by 87 percent.

Some scientists call this insect Armageddon. It sounds more like a video game, except it's a serious result of climate change, pesticides, and the loss of meadows with a variety of plants. The immediate impact is a real-life threat to the world's food supply. One way to increase pollinators is to seed areas with diverse plants and flowers. It is likely that monoculture of crops has deprived bees and other pollinators of both habitat and food. Maybe crop yields could be improved by setting some land aside for a pollinator ecosystem adjacent to the groves of almonds or the fields of corn. I like to find solutions to problems where both the land and the farmer can benefit.

Last summer, I was at an animal behavior conference with a group of people, standing around. My leg started to hurt so I moved off to the side to sit on some steps. It was then I spotted a busy hive of activity off to my side. It was early afternoon, and I noticed a patch of dirt that had plants growing on it. It was an abandoned piece of land that was now covered with wildflowers, morning glories. White and yellow moths were dancing around the flowers, pollinating them. Then at another location, in between two fences, I noticed some purple sage that had attracted tons of honeybees and yellow jackets. This whole world came to life in front of me, and I knew that if it had been a couple of hours later, when the sun was lower in the sky, the flowers would have closed up and the whole display would have been gone. It was a brief window during which I witnessed a frenzy of activity and pollination. And all this on patches of forgotten dirt.

Whenever I drive to the airport, I see a huge pile of sand on the side of the road. The sand was piled up so it could be used for road and bridge construction. It always catches my eye because it's so enormous. One day, driving home, I noticed some green shoots coming out of the dirt. For the rest of the summer, every time I drove by, I'd see more and more green growth on this mountain of sand. It got me thinking about the relationship between the earth and all living things, and about the ability of living things to rejuvenate or come back to life.

Thirty years ago, at Chernobyl in Ukraine, there was the worst nuclear disaster in history. All the people were evacuated. The trees turned the color of rust and were named the Red Forest. Humans are no longer allowed to live there, but something interesting is happening with the wildlife. Animals are coming back: bears, moose, foxes, lynx, and beavers are returning. As are fish, worms, and bacteria in the water. This means that there is clean food and a water supply for the animals to thrive. This once-destroyed area is coming back to life. A photographer named Jonathan "Jonk" Jimenez photographed plants taking over deserted buildings in his book *Naturalia: Reclaimed by Nature*. There is a really cool website (organics.org/30-must-see-breathtaking-places-reclaimed-by-nature) where you can see incredible pictures of places that have been reclaimed by nature, including schools, hotels, trains and roller coasters. They are covered with leaves, moss, sand, and vegetation and worn by wind and weather. Recently I talked to a man who had to tear down a factory that had been abandoned for fifteen years. It was full of life. One room had become home to numerous owls. Nature comes back. Life returns.

The best way to get involved, the way I've lived my life, is doing projects. From my childhood activities to the work I do with animals today, it all starts with an idea, with wanting to figure out how things work, how to make life better for us, for animals, and for the environment. Getting out there and getting involved. That's why I'm so excited by all the citizen science projects going on today. You don't have to be a professor or a professional, just someone who cares about the environment. You can share data on everything from birds to bugs, in cities and rural areas.

A great backyard bird count is conducted during the third week of

February when people around the globe report on the birds in their area. You can collect information on frogs at FrogWatch USA and report on ladybugs. Their numbers have fallen over the last twenty years, and groups of citizen scientists have been hunting for them and uploading pictures to a public database. Some groups are collecting water samples to test for bacteria, while others are collecting dragonfly larvae to analyze the level of mercury contamination. In my own hometown of Fort Collins, Colorado, a group of citizen scientists has formed to collect data on bee diversity called Native Bee Watch. As pollinators, bees impact 35 percent of global crops, including fruits and vegetables, and the bee population has decreased approximately 40 percent. We need to learn what's happening, and citizen scientists are answering the call.

Roger Tory Peterson said that the best way to get people to become environmental problem-solvers is to teach them about nature. I hope that the first experiences every child has of nature are like the ones that I had growing up, filled with wonderment and fun. I tried to share those experiences here, and how they sparked a deeper love of learning. I hope that you might consider a career in animal science, or geology, or even dendrochronology. That you will come to closely observe nature and think about how to save a stream, or slow the icebergs from melting, or keep the bumblebees from disappearing. It's clear we need more scientists, people who are in the field, working with nature to help protect our beautiful planet. What has given my life meaning is more than doing science; it's helping people solve problems using science. Doing something that makes a difference with what I've learned. It all begins with observation. Seeing what others don't see.

ACKNOWLEDGMENTS

The author would like to thank the following people for their hands-on help with this project: Krista Ahlberg, Talia Benamy, Wendy Dopkin, Marc Greenawalt, Kenton Hoppas, Vivian Kirklin, Cheryl Miller, Jill Santopolo, Monique Sterling, and Marinda Valenti.

BIBLIOGRAPHY

Ackerman, Jennifer. *The Genius of Birds*. New York: Penguin, 2016.

Adams, Tim. "Natural Talent." *The Guardian*, March 10, 2007.

Agenbroad, Larry D., and Rhodes W. Fairbridge. "Holocene Epoch." *Encyclopaedia Britannica*. https://www.britannica.com/science/Holocene-Epoch.

Alden, Andrew. "10 Steps for Easy Mineral Identification." ThoughtCo. Updated September 5, 2019. https://www.thoughtco.com/how-to-identify-minerals-1440936.

Andersen, Geoff. *The Telescope: Its History, Technology and Future*. Princeton, N.J.: Princeton University Press, 2007.

"Andrew E. Douglass: Father of Dendrochronology." University of Arizona Laboratory of Tree-Ring Research. https://www.ltrr.arizona.edu/~cbaisan/Vermont/Erica/AED.pdf.

"Andy Goldsworthy—Biography and Legacy." The Art Story. https://www.theartstory.org/artist-goldsworthy-andy-life-and-legacy.htm.

Atkinson, Joe. "From Computers to Leaders: Women at NASA Langley." NASA. March 27, 2014. https://www.nasa.gov/larc/from-computers-to-leaders-women-at-nasa-langley.

Attenborough, David. *The Life of Birds*. Princeton, N.J.: Princeton University Press, 1998.

Azvolinsky, Anna. "Singing in the Brain." *The Scientist*, March 1, 2017.

Ball, Philip. "These Are the Discoveries That Made Stephen Hawking Famous." BBC. January 7, 2016. http://www.bbc.com/earth story/20160107-these-are-the-discoveries-that-made-stephen-hawking-famous.

Ballard, Robert, with Will Hively. *The Eternal Darkness: A Personal History of Deep Sea Exploration.* Princeton, N.J.: Princeton University Press, 2000.

"Barn Swallow." The Cornell Lab of Ornithology: All About Birds. https://www.allaboutbirds.org /guide/Barn_Swallow/overview.

Barnard, Anne. "How a Rooftop Meadow of Bees and Butterflies Shows New York City's Future." *The New York Times*, October 26, 2019.

Barnes, Simon. *The Meaning of Birds*. New York: Pegasus, 2018.

Barrow, Mark. *A Passion for Birds*. Princeton, N.J.: Princeton University Press, 1998.

Bartels, Meghan. "The Unbelievable Life of the Forgotten Genius Who Turned Americans' Space Dreams into Reality." *Business Insider*, August 22, 2016. https://www.businessinsider.com /katherine-johnson-hidden-figures-nasa-human-computers-2016-8.

Basinet, Alan. "Marble Alan's Encyclopedia Marble Reference Archive!" https://www .kingofalltechnology.com/basinetmarbleinformation.htm.

Battista, Carolyn. "Stone Walls, Clues to a Very Deep Past." *The New York Times*, September 27, 1998.

Benedict, Carey. "Alex, a Parrot Who Had a Way with Words, Dies." *The New York Times*, September 10, 2007.

Bennett, Jeffrey, et al. *The Cosmic Perspective*: *The Solar System*. San Francisco: Addison Wesley, 2007.

"Big Audubon Prints Soar to a Market High." Auction Central News. November 22, 2010. https://www.liveauctioneers.com/news/features/freelancewriter/big-audubon-prints -soar-to-a-market-high/.

Bjork, Daniel W. *B. F. Skinner: A Life*. New York: Basic, 1993.

Bohannon, John. "Sunflowers Show Complex Fibonacci Sequences." *Science*, May 17, 2016.

The Book of Record of the Time Capsule of Cupaloy. New York: Westinghouse Electric & Manufacturing Company, 1938. https://archive.org/details/timecapsulecups00westrich.

Botique, Laura R., et al. "Ancient European Dog Genomes Reveal Continuity Since the Early Neolithic." *Nature Communications* 16082 (2017).

Boyle, J. H., H. J. Dalgleish, and J. R. Puzey. "Monarch Butterfly and Milkweed Declines Substantially Predate the Use of Genetically Modified Crops." *Proceedings of the National Academy of Sciences* 116, no. 8 (2019): 3006–11.

Breashears, David, and Audrey Salkeld. *Last Climb: The Legendary Everest Expeditions of George Mallory.* New York: National Geographic, 1999.

Breland, Keller, and Marian Breland. "The Misbehavior of Organisms." *American Psychologist* 16 (1961): 681–84.

Broad, William J. "Even in Death, Carl Sagan's Influence Is Still Cosmic." *The New York Times,* December 1, 1998.

Broad, William J. "Wreckage of Titanic Reported Discovered 12,000 Feet Down." *The New York Times,* September 3, 1985. https://www.nytimes.com/1985/09/03/science/wreckage-of -titanic-reported-discovered-12000-feet-down.html.

Brown, Paul. "The Life-and-Death History of the Message in a Bottle." Medium. September 30, 2016. https://medium.com/@paulbrownUK/the-life-and-death-history-of-the-message -in-a-bottle-65e9dc6bf41f.

Bucci, Amy. "Explorer of the Week: Jill Pruetz." *Explorer's Journal,* October 18, 2012.

Burakoff, Maddie. "Decoding the Mathematical Secrets of Plants' Stunning Leaf Patterns." *Smithsonian Magazine,* June 4, 2019.

Burnie, David. *How Nature Works.* New York: DK, 1991.

Buzhardt, Lynn. "Search and Rescue Dogs." VCA Hospitals. https://vcahospitals.com/know-your -pet/search-and-rescue-dogs.

Carson, Rachel. *Silent Spring.* New York: Mariner, 2002. (Originally published 1962.)

Carson, Rachel. *Under the Sea-Wind.* New York: Penguin, 1996. (Originally published 1941.)

Cepelewicz, Jordana. "In Birds' Songs, Brains and Genes, He Finds Clues to Speech." *Quanta Magazine,* January 30, 2018.

Chambers, Joseph R. *Concept to Reality: Contributions of the NASA Langley Research Center to U.S. Civil Aircraft of the 1990s.* Report No. SP-2003-4529 (Yorktown, VA: NASA, 2003). https://history.nasa.gov/monograph29.pdf.

Conley, Andrea. *Window on the Deep: The Adventures of Underwater Explorer Sylvia Earle.* New York: Franklin Watts, 1991.

Crouch, Tom D. "Wright Brothers." *Encyclopaedia Britannica.* Updated March 4, 2020. https://www.britannica.com/biography/Wright-brothers.

Darwin, Charles. *On the Origin of Species.* New York: Modern Library, 1998. (Originally published 1859.)

"David Sibley Online." Surfbirds.com. http://www.surfbirds.com/Features/sibleyonline.html.

Davidson, Keay. *Carl Sagan: A Life.* New York: John Wiley & Sons, 1999.

Davis, Gareth Huw. "Parenthood." PBS. https://www.pbs.org/lifeofbirds/home/index.html.

"The Day That Stephen Hawking Soared Like Superman." BBC News. March 17, 2018. https://www.bbc.com/news/in-pictures-43430023.

de Monchaux, Nicholas. *Space Suit: Fashioning Apollo.* Cambridge, Mass.: MIT Press, 2011.

de Waal, Frans. *Are We Smart Enough to Know How Smart Animals Are?* New York: W. W. Norton, 2017.

de Waal, Frans. "The Brains of the Animal Kingdom." *Wall Street Journal*, March 22, 2013. https://www.wsj.com/articles/SB10001424127887323869604578370574285382756.

de Waal, Frans. "Darwin's Last Laugh." *Nature* 460 (July 9, 2009): 175.

de Waal, Frans. *Mama's Last Hug: Animal Emotions and What They Tell Us About Ourselves.* New York: W. W. Norton, 2019.

DeVorkin, David H., and Robert W. Smith. *Hubble: Imaging Space and Time.* Washington, D.C.: National Geographic, 2013.

di Paolo, Jon. "Crew Capsule Designed to Take US Astronauts Back to Moon Completed." *The Independent*, July 21, 2019. https://www.independent.co.uk/news/world/americas/moon-mission-nasa-apollo-11-artemis-orion-kennedy-center-a9014031.html.

Diamond, Anna. "Why Are Starfish Shaped Like Stars and More Questions from Our Readers." *Smithsonian Magazine*, January 2019. https://www.smithsonianmag.com/smithsonian -institution/why-starfish-shaped-stars-180971008/.

Donavan, James. *Shoot for the Moon*. New York: Little, Brown, 2019.

"Dr. Edward C. Stone (1936–)." Jet Propulsion Laboratory, California Institute of Technology, NASA. https://www.jpl.nasa.gov/about/bio_stone.php.

Drake, Nadia. "When Hubble Stared at Nothing for 100 Hours." *National Geographic*, April 24, 2015.

Dreifus, Claudia. "A Conversation with Erich Jarvis: A Biologist Explores the Minds of Birds That Learn to Sing." *The New York Times*, January 7, 2003.

Dreifus, Claudia. "Life and the Cosmos, Word by Painstaking Word." *The New York Times*, May 9, 2011.

Earle, Sylvia. *Blue Hope: Exploring and Caring for Earth's Magnificent Ocean*. Washington, D.C.: National Geographic, 2014.

Earle, Sylvia. "The Lorax Who Speaks for the Fishes." *Radcliffe Quarterly*, September 1990.

Ebbesmeyer, Curtis, and Eric Scigliano. *Flotsametrics and the Floating World*. Washington, D.C.: Smithsonian, 2009.

Ebbesmeyer, Curtis. "Beachcombing Science from Bath Toys." Beachcombers' Alert! http://beachcombersalert.org/RubberDuckies.html.

Emling, Shelley. *The Fossil Hunter: Dinosaurs, Evolution, and the Woman Who Changed Science*. New York: Griffin, 2009.

"Eugene Shoemaker." Famous Scientists. https://www.famousscientists.org/gene-shoemaker/.

Fishman, Charles. "The Improbable Story of the Bra-maker Who Won the Right to Make Astronaut Spacesuits." *Fast Company*, July 15, 2019. https://www.fastcompany.com/90375440 /the-improbable-story-of-the-bra-maker-who-won-the-right-to-make-astronaut-spacesuits.

"Fossil." *National Geographic*. https://www.nationalgeographic.org/encyclopedia/fossil/.

Fox, Margalit. "Gary Dahl, Inventor of Pet Rock, Dies at 78." *The New York Times*, March 31, 2015.

Frantz, Laurent A. F., et al. "Genomic and Archaeological Evidence Suggest a Dual Origin of Domestic Dogs." *Science* 352 (2016): 1228–31.

Garner, Rob. "About the Hubble Space Telescope." NASA. https://www.nasa.gov/mission_pages /hubble/story/index.html.

Gaudin, Sharon. "NASA's Apollo Technology Has Changed History." *Computerworld*, July 20, 2009. https://www.computerworld.com/article/2525898/nasa-s-apollo-technology-has-changed -history.html.

Gelt, Jessica. "The $8 Million Audubon Book About Birds, and the Amazing Story Behind It." *Los Angeles Times*, May 31, 2018.

"Geode." *Encyclopaedia Britannica*. https://www.britannica.com/science/geode.

Gerbis, Nicholas. "How Are Crystals Made?" HowStuffWorks.com. March 13, 2013. https://science .howstuffworks.com/environmental/earth/geology/how-are-crystals-made.htm.

Gershwin, Lisa-Ann. *Jellyfish: A Natural History.* Chicago: University of Chicago Press, 2016.

Ghosh, Pallab. "Hawking Urges Moon Landing to 'Elevate Humanity.'" BBC News. June 20, 2017 https://www.bbc.com/news/science-environment-40345048.

Globe at Night. "Six Easy Star Hunting Steps." National Optical Astronomy Observatory: Globe at Night. https://www.globeatnight.org/6-steps.php.

Godin, Alfred J. "Birds at Airports." *The Handbook: Prevention and Control of Wildlife Damage* 56. January 1994. https://digitalcommons.unl.edu/icwdmhandbook/56/.

Goldsworthy, Andy. *Projects.* New York: Abrams, 2017.

Goodall, Jane, and Phillip Berman. *Reason for Hope.* New York: Hachette, 1999.

Goodall, Jane. *Hope for Animals and Their World.* New York: Grand Central, 2009.

Goodall, Jane. *In the Shadow of Man.* New York: Mariner, 2010.

Goulson, D., et al. "Bee Declines Driven by Combined Stress from Parasites, Pesticides, and Lack of Flowers." *Science* 347, no. 6229 (2015): 1255957.

Green, Dan. *Rocks and Minerals.* New York: Scholastic, 2013.

Green, Dan. *The Smithsonian Rock and Gem Book*. New York: DK, 2016.

Green, Michelle. "Stephen Jay Gould." *People*. June 2, 1986. https://people.com/archive
/stephen-jay-gould-vol-25-no-22/.

Grimm, David. "Earliest Evidence for Dog Breeding Found on Remote Siberian Island." *Science*,
December 8, 2017. https://www.sciencemag.org/news/2017/05/earliest-evidence-dog
-breeding-found-remote-siberian-island.

Gugliotta, Guy. "Historic Voyager Mission May Lose Its Funding." *Washington Post*, April 4, 2005.

Hand, Justine. "Summertime DIY: Pressed Seaweed Prints." Gardenista. June 28, 2019. https://
www.gardenista.com/posts/pressed-seaweed-prints/.

Handwerk, Brian. "How Accurate Is *Alpha*'s Theory of Dog Domestication?" *Smithsonian
Magazine*, August 15, 2018. https://www.smithsonianmag.com/science-nature/how
-wolves-really-became-dogs-180970014/.

Hare, Brian, and Vanessa Woods. *The Genius of Dogs: How Dogs Are Smarter Than You Think*. New
York: Dutton, 2013.

Harrison, Hal H. *A Field Guide to Western Birds' Nests: Of 520 Species Found Breeding in the United
States West of the Mississippi River*. Boston: Houghton Mifflin, 1979.

Hawking, Stephen. *A Brief History of Time*. New York: Bantam, 1998.

Hawking, Stephen. *My Brief History*. New York: Bantam, 2013.

Haynes, Suyin. "'Now I Am Speaking to the Whole World.' How Teen Climate Activist Greta
Thunberg Got Everyone to Listen." *Time*, May 16, 2019.

"History & Archives." Jet Propulsion Laboratory, California Institute of Technology, NASA. https://
www.jpl.nasa.gov/about/history.php.

Hohn, Donovan. *Moby-Duck: The True Story of 28,800 Bath Toys Lost at Sea and of the Beachcombers,
Oceanographers, Environmentalists, and Fools, Including the Author, Who Went in Search of Them*.
New York: Penguin, 2012.

Hollingham, Richard. "Voyager: Inside the World's Greatest Space Mission." BBC Future. August
18, 2017. https://www.bbc.com/future/article/20170818-voyager-inside-the-worlds-greatest
-space-mission.

Horne, Francis. "How Are Seashells Created? Or Any Other Shell, Such as a Snail's or a Turtle's?" *Scientific American*, October 23, 2006. https://www.scientificamerican.com/article/how-are-seashells-created/.

"Horseshoe Crab." *Encyclopaedia Britannica*. https://www.britannica.com/animal/horseshoe-crab.

"Horseshoe Crab." National Wildlife Federation. https://www.nwf.org/Educational-Resources/Wildlife-Guide/Invertebrates/Horseshoe-Crab.

Hotz, Robert Lee. "An Apollo Spacecraft Computer Is Brought Back to Life." *Wall Street Journal*, July 14, 2019.

"How Do Hurricanes Form?" NASA Science Space Place, NASA. Updated December 4, 2019. https://spaceplace.nasa.gov/hurricanes/en/.

"How Does A Stone 'Skip' Across Water?" Library of Congress. https://www.loc.gov/rr/scitech/mysteries/stoneskip.html.

"How Does Sand Form?" National Oceanic and Atmospheric Administration. https://oceanservice.noaa.gov/facts/sand.html.

Hsu, Tiffany. "The Apollo 11 Mission Was Also a Global Media Sensation." *The New York Times*, July 15, 2019.

Hynes, Margaret. *Rocks and Fossils*. Boston: Kingfisher, 2006.

Jacobo, Julia. "Nearly 40% Decline in Honey Bee Population Last Winter 'Unsustainable,' Experts Say." ABC News. July 9, 2019. https://abcnews.go.com/US/40-decline-honey-bee-population-winter-unsustainable-experts/story?id=64191609.

Jaramillo, Alvaro. "Understanding the Basics of Bird Molts." Audubon. November 16, 2017. https://www.audubon.org/news/understanding-basics-bird-molts.

Jarvis, Brooke. "The Insect Apocalypse Is Here." *The New York Times Magazine*, November 27, 2018.

Jarvis, Erich D. "Evolution of Vocal Learning and Spoken Language." *Science* 366, no. 6461 (2019): 50–54.

"Johann Rudolf Wyss." *Encyclopaedia Britannica*. Updated March 17, 2020. https://www.britannica.com/biography/Johann-Rudolf-Wyss#ref185179.

"John James Audubon." Audubon. https://www.audubon.org/content/john-james-audubon.

"John James Audubon." National Gallery of Art. https://www.nga.gov/collection/artist-info.122
.html.

"Johnny Appleseed." *Encyclopaedia Britannica*. Updated March 16, 2020. https://www.britannica
.com/biography/John-Chapman.

Johnson, George. "Alex Wanted a Cracker, but Did He Want One?" *The New York Times*,
September 16, 2007.

Jonas, Gerald. "Jacques Cousteau, Oceans' Impresario, Dies." *The New York Times*, June 26, 1997.
https://www.nytimes.com/1997/06/26/world/jacques-cousteau-oceans-impresario-dies.html.

Kane, Sean. "Most Dog Breeds Emerged from a Shockingly Recent Moment in History." *Business
Insider*, February 25, 2016. https://www.businessinsider.com/dog-breeds-victorian-england
-origins-2016-2.

"Katherine Johnson: The Girl Who Loved to Count." NASA. November 24, 2015. https://www
.nasa.gov/feature/katherine-johnson-the-girl-who-loved-to-count.

Kennedy, Jennifer. "All About the Jingle Shell." ThoughtCo. Updated May 30, 2019. https://www
.thoughtco.com/jingle-shell-profile-2291802.

Kieffer, Susan W. "Eugene M. Shoemaker." National Academy of Sciences. 2015. http://www
.nasonline.org/publications/biographical-memoirs/memoir-pdfs/shoemaker-eugene.pdf.

The King of Random. "Turn Apple Seeds into a Tree." YouTube. May 11, 2017. Video, 3:39. https://
www.youtube.com/watch?v=Wc3T1ig0n6U.

King, Bob. "How to See and Photograph Geosynchronous Satellites." *Sky and Telescope*, September
20, 2017.

King, David. *Charles Darwin*. London: DK, 2007.

Krull, Kathleen. *Charles Darwin*. New York: Viking, 2010.

Kusmer, Anna. "New England Is Crisscrossed with Thousands of Miles of Stone Walls." Atlas
Obscura. May 4, 2018. https://www.atlasobscura.com/articles/new-england-stone-walls.

Lammle, Rob. "A Brief History of Marbles (Including All That Marble Slang)." Mental Floss. November 3, 2015. http://mentalfloss.com/article/29486/brief-history-marbles-including -all-marble-slang.

Law, Kara Lavender. "Plastics in the Environment." *Annual Review of Marine Science* 9 (2017): 205–29.

Lear, Linda. *Rachel Carson: Witness for Nature*. New York: Henry Holt, 1997.

Levy, David H. *Shoemaker by Levy: The Man Who Made an Impact.* Princeton, N.J.: Princeton University Press, 2000.

Libby, Heather. "It's the Hubble Telescope's Most Famous Image. Here's How It Almost Didn't Happen." Upworthy. August 12, 2016.

"The Life and Legacy of Rachel Carson." Rachel Carson. http://www.rachelcarson.org/.

"Light Pollution." International Dark-Sky Association. February 14, 2017. https://www.darksky .org/light-pollution/.

Louv, Richard. *Last Child in the Woods*. Chapel Hill, N.C.: Algonquin, 2005.

"Lyme Regis Fossils." Lyme Regis. http://www.lymeregis.org/fossils.aspx.

Main, Douglas. "Most People Believe Intelligent Aliens Exist, Poll Says." *Newsweek*, September 29, 2015. https://www.newsweek.com/most-people-believe-intelligent-aliens-exist-377965.

Main, Douglas. "Why Insect Populations Are Plummeting and Why It Matters." *National Geographic*, February 14, 2019.

Martínez, I., F. Jutglar, and E.F.J. Garcia. "King Penguin (*Aptenodytes patagonicus*)." Cornell Lab of Ornithology: Birds of the World. https://birdsoftheworld.org/bow/species/kinpen1/cur /introduction.

"Mary Anning." Lyme Regis. http://www.lymeregis.org/mary-anning.aspx.

Mason, Lisa, and H. S. Arathi. "Assessing the Efficacy of Citizen Scientists Monitoring Native Bees in Urban Areas." *Global Ecology and Conservation* 17 (January 2019).

Matsen, Brad. *Jacques Cousteau: The Sea King.* New York: Vintage, 2009.

McCarthy, Michael. "World's Greatest Birdwatcher Sets a New Record—Then Hangs Up His Binoculars." *The Independent*, October 15, 2012.

McGraw, Donald J. "Andrew Ellicott Douglass and the Big Trees: The Giant Sequoia Was Fundamental to the Development of the Science of Dendrochronology—Tree-Ring Dating." *American Scientist*, September–October 2000.

McKie, Robin. "Rachel Carson and the Legacy of Silent Spring." *The Guardian*, May 26, 2012.

"Mohs Hardness." *Encyclopaedia Britannica*. https://www.britannica.com/science/Mohs-hardness.

"Monarch Butterflies." University of Wisconsin–Madison Arboretum. https://journeynorth.org /monarchs.

Mosher, Dave. "Elon Musk Says SpaceX Could Land on the Moon in 2 Years." *Business Insider*, July 24, 2019. https://www.businessinsider.com/spacex-elon-musk-moon-landing -nasa-cfo-jeff-dewit-2019-7.

Mulligan, Annie. "How to Tell the Age of a Tree Without Cutting It Down." Hunker. https://www .hunker.com/12001364/how-to-tell-the-age-of-a-tree-without-cutting-it-down.

Musil, Robert K. *Rachel Carson and Her Sisters.* New Brunswick, N.J.: Rutgers University Press, 2014.

"NASA Spacecraft Embarks on Historic Journey into Interstellar Space." Jet Propulsion Laboratory, California Institute of Technology, NASA. September 12, 2013. https://www.jpl .nasa.gov/news/news.php?release=2013-277.

National Geographic Society. *Illustrated Guide to Nature: From Your Back Door to the Great Outdoors: Wildflowers, Trees & Shrubs, Rocks & Minerals, Weather, Night Sky.* New York: National Geographic, 2013.

Nelson, Bryan. "What Can 28,000 Rubber Duckies Lost at Sea Tell Us About Our Oceans?" MNN. March 1, 2011. https://www.mnn.com/earth-matters/wilderness-resources/stories /what-can-28000-rubber-duckies-lost-at-sea-teach-us-about.

The New York Times Editorial Board. "Rendezvous with Pluto." *The New York Times*, July 16, 2015.

"1939 Westinghouse Time Capsule Complete List Contents." *The New York Times*. https://archive .nytimes.com/www.nytimes.com/specials/magazine3/items.html.

"Nurdle Patrol." University of Texas at Austin Nurdle Patrol. nurdlepatrol.org.

Nuwer, Rachel. "How to Find a Four-Leaf Clover." *Smithsonian Magazine*, March 17, 2014. https://www.smithsonianmag.com/smart-news/how-find-four-leaf-clover-180950114/.

Overbye, Dennis. "Stephen Hawking Dies at 76; His Mind Roamed the Cosmos." *The New York Times*, March 14, 2018.

Pellant, Chris. *Rocks and Minerals*. London: DK, 1992.

Pennisi, Elizabeth. "Three Billion North American Birds Have Vanished Since 1970, Surveys Show." *Science*, September 19, 2019.

Pepperberg, Irene M. *Alex & Me*. New York: Harper, 2008.

Perimeter Institute. "14 Mind-Bogglingly Awesome Facts About the Hubble Deep Field Images." *Inside the Perimeter*. January 28, 2020.

Peterson, Dale. *Jane Goodall: The Woman Who Redefined Man*. New York: Houghton Mifflin, 2006.

Petruzzello, Melissa. "Can Apple Seeds Kill You?" *Encyclopaedia Britannica*. https://www.britannica.com/story/can-apple-seeds-kill-you.

Petsko, Gregory A. "The Blue Marble." *Genome Biology* 12, no. 4 (April 2011).

"The Physics of Sandcastles." NASA Science, NASA. July 11, 2002. https://science.nasa.gov/science-news/science-at-nasa/2002/11jul_mgm.

Pilley, John W. *Chaser: Unlocking the Genius of a Dog Who Knows a Thousand Words*. New York: Houghton Mifflin Harcourt, 2013.

Pollan, Michael. *The Botany of Desire*. New York: Random House, 2001.

Powers, Anna. "The Theory of Everything: Remembering Stephen Hawking's Greatest Contribution." *Forbes*, March 14, 2018.

"Primatologist Frans de Waal Explores Animal Emotions." *Science Friday*. March 15, 2019. https://www.sciencefriday.com/segments/primatologist-frans-de-waal-explores-animal-emotions/.

Pruetz, Jill. "Rescued Fongoli Chimp Baby Reunited with Her Mother." *NatGeo News Watch*. January 29, 2009.

Pyle, Rod. "Apollo 11's Scariest Moments: Perils of the First Manned Moon Landing." Space.com. July 21, 2014. https://www.space.com/26593-apollo-11-moon-landing-scariest-moments.html.

"Rachel Carson Biography." U.S. Fish and Wildlife Service. Updated February 5, 2013. https://www.fws.gov/refuge/rachel_carson/about/rachelcarson.html.

Rafferty, John P. "Mary Anning." *Encyclopaedia Britannica*. Updated March 5, 2020. https://www.britannica.com/biography/Mary-Anning.

Reich, Peter A. *Language Development*. Englewood Cliffs, N.J.: Prentice-Hall, 1986.

Reser, Jared Edward. "Solitary Mammals Provide an Animal Model for Autism Spectrum." *Journal of Comparative Psychology* 128, no. 1 (February 2002): 99–113. https://psycnet.apa.org/buy/2013-38545-001.

Rhodes, Christopher, J. "Plastic Pollution and Potential Solutions." *Science Progress* 101, no. 3 (2018): 207–60.

Rhodes, Christopher, J. "Pollinator Decline—An Ecological Calamity in the Making?" *Science Progress* 101, no. 2 (2018): 121–60.

Rhodes, Richard. *John James Audubon: The Making of an American*. New York: Knopf, 2004.

Ridley, Glynis. *The Discovery of Jeanne Baret: A Story of Science, the High Seas, and the First Woman to Circumnavigate the Globe*. New York: Crown, 2010.

Robbins, Jim. "Chronicle of the Rings." *The New York Times*, April 20, 2019.

Robbins, Jim. *The Wonder of Birds*. New York: Spiegel & Grau, 2017.

"Robert D. Ballard." Nautilus Live. https://nautiluslive.org/people/robert-ballard.

"Roger Tory Peterson Biography." Roger Tory Peterson Institute of Natural History. https://rtpi.org/roger-tory-peterson/roger-tory-peterson-biography/.

Rosen, Jonathan. "The Difference between Bird Watching and Birding." *The New Yorker*, October 17, 2011.

Rothman, Julia. *Nature Anatomy: The Curious Parts and Pieces of the Natural World*. North Adams, M.A.: Storey, 2015.

Rowland, Scott K., and R. S. J. Sparks. "A Pictorial Summary of the Life and Work of George Patrick Leonard Walker." In *Studies in Volcanology: The Legacy of George Walker*, edited by T. Thordarson, S. Self, G. Larsen, S. K. Rowland, and Á. Höskuldsson, 371-400. London: The Geological Society, 2009.

Sagan, Carl. *Cosmos*. New York: Random House, 1980.

Sagan, Carl. *Murmurs of Earth: The Voyager Interstellar Record*. New York: Random House, 1978.

Schwartz, John. "Decline of Pollinators Poses Threat to World Food Supply." *The New York Times*, February 26, 2016.

Self, S., and R. S. J. Sparks. "George Patrick Leonard Walker." *Biographical Memoirs of Fellows of the Royal Society* 52 (2006): 423–36.

"Shaw Prize in Astronomy Awarded to Ed Stone." Jet Propulsion Laboratory, California Institute of Technology, NASA. May 22, 2019.

Shetterly, Margot Lee. *Hidden Figures: The American Dream and the Untold Story of the Black Women Mathematicians Who Helped Win the Space Race*. New York: William Morrow, 2016.

Sibley, David Allen. *The Sibley Guide to Bird Life and Behavior*. New York: Knopf, 2000.

60 Minutes Australia. "Extra Minutes: Interview with Dr. Ed Stone." YouTube. August 4, 2013. https://www.youtube.com/watch?v=vJ1sKKQQKQc.

Skinner, B. F. *Particulars of My Life*. New York: Knopf, 1976.

Smith, Dinitia, "A Thinking Bird or Just Another Bird Brain?" *The New York Times*, October 9, 1999.

Smith, PD. "Dinosaur in a Haystack by Stephen Jay Gould—Review." *The Guardian,* November 15, 2011.

Smithsonian. *Natural History: The Ultimate Visual Guide to Everything on Earth*. London: DK, 2010.

Soniak, Matt. "Why Do Shells Sound Like the Ocean?" Mental Floss. August 20, 2009. http://mentalfloss.com/article/22573/why-do-shells-sound-ocean.

Souder, William. "How Two Women Ended the Deadly Feather Trade." *Smithsonian Magazine*, March 2013.

Spivack, Emily. "What Did Playtex Have to Do with Neil Armstrong?" *Smithsonian Magazine*, August 27, 2012. https://www.smithsonianmag.com/arts-culture/what-did-playtex-have-to-do-with-neil-armstrong-16588944/.

"Sputnik 1." NASA. October 4, 2011. https://www.nasa.gov/multimedia/imagegallery/image_feature_924.html.

"Sputnik and the Dawn of the Space Age." NASA. https://history.nasa.gov/sputnik/.

St. Fleur, Nicholas. "Colorado Fossils Show How Mammals Raced to Fill Dinosaurs' Void." *The New York Times*, October 24, 2019. https://www.nytimes.com/2019/10/24/science/fossils-mammals-dinosaurs-colorado.html.

"Starfish Facts!" *National Geographic Kids*. https://www.natgeokids.com/uk/discover/animals/sea-life/starfish-facts/.

"Starfish (Sea Stars)." *National Geographic*. https://www.nationalgeographic.com/animals/invertebrates/group/starfish/.

Stierwalt, Sabrina. "How Does Sand Get Its Color?" Quick and Dirty Tips. January 29, 2018. https://www.quickanddirtytips.com/education/science/how-does-sand-get-its-color?.

Stockton, Nick. "The Mysterious Genetics of the Four-Leaf Clover." *Wired*, March 17, 2015. https://www.wired.com/2015/03/mysterious-genetics-four-leaf-clover/.

Stowell, Lauren. "The 18th Century Dog." *American Duchess* (blog), February 17, 2010. http://blog.americanduchess.com/2010/02/18th-century-dog.html.

Stuart, S. C. "40 Years of Voyager: A Q&A with Dr. Ed Stone at NASA JPL." *PCMag*, March 4, 2017.

Surridge, Christopher. "Leaves by Number." *Nature* 426 (2003): 237.

Taylor, Alan. "The 1939 New York World's Fair." *The Atlantic*, November 01, 2013. https://www.theatlantic.com/photo/2013/11/the-1939-new-york-worlds-fair/100620/.

Temming, Maria. "Tiny Plastic Debris Is Accumulating Far beneath the Ocean Surface." *Science News*, June 6, 2019.

"10 Facts About Stephen Hawking!" *National Geographic Kids*. https://www.natgeokids.com/za/discover/science/general-science/stephen-hawking-facts/.

Thomas, Elizabeth Marshall. *The Hidden Life of Dogs.* Boston: Mariner, 2010.

Tingley, Kim. "The Loyal Engineers Steering NASA's Voyager Probes Across the Universe." *The New York Times*, August 3, 2017.

Tomecek, Steve. *Rocks and Minerals.* Washington, D.C.: National Geographic, 2010.

Torrens, Hugh. "Presidential Address: Mary Anning (1799-1847) of Lyme; 'The Greatest Fossilist the World Ever Knew.'" *The British Journal for the History of Science* 28, no. 3 (1995): 257-84. www.jstor.org/stable/4027645.

Tudge, Colin. *The Tree: A Natural History of What Trees Are, How They Live, and Why They Matter.* New York: Three Rivers, 2007.

Tyson, Neil Degrasse. *Astrophysics for People in a Hurry.* New York: W. W. Norton, 2018.

Tyson, Peter. "Dogs' Dazzling Sense of Smell." PBS. October 4, 2012. https://www.pbs.org/wgbh /nova/article/dogs-sense-of-smell/.

Vanderhoff, N., et al. "American Robin (*Turdus migratorius*)." March 4, 2020. The Cornell Lab of Ornithology: Birds of the World.

Viteli, Romeo. "What Can Solitary Mammals Teach Us About Autism?" *Psychology Today*, June 2, 2014. https://www.psychologytoday.com/us/blog/media-spotlight/201406/what-can-solitary -mammals-teach-us-about-autism.

Wadge, Geoff. "George Walker." *The Guardian*, February 21, 2005.

Weaver, H. A. "The Activity and Size of the Nucleus of Comet Hale-Bopp (C/1995 O1)." *Science* 275, no. 5308 (March 28, 1997): 1900–04.

"Webb vs Hubble Telescope." James Webb Space Telescope, NASA. https://jwst.nasa.gov/content /about/comparisonWebbVsHubble.html.

"What Is Artemis?" NASA. July 25, 2019. https://www.nasa.gov/what-is-artemis.

"What Is the Size of a Comet?" Cool Cosmos. http://coolcosmos.ipac.caltech.edu /ask/182-What-is-the-size-of-a-comet-.

Wilkins, Alasdair. "How NASA Fights to Keep Dying Spacecraft Alive." *Scientific American*, October 24, 2016. https://www.scientificamerican.com/article/how-nasa-fights-to-keep -dying-spacecraft-alive/.

Williams, David B. "Benchmarks: September 30, 1861: Archaeopteryx Is Discovered and Described." *Earth*, September 2, 2011. https://www.earthmagazine.org/article /benchmarks-september-30-1861-archaeopteryx-discovered-and-described.

Wilson, Edward O. *Naturalist*. New York: Warner, 1995.

Witt, Stephen. "Apollo 11: Mission Out of Control." *Wired*, June 24, 2019.

Wyss, Johann. *The Swiss Family Robinson*. New York: Doubleday, 1989. (Originally published 1812.)

ARTICLES BY THE AUTHOR

Coppola, Christa L., Temple Grandin, and Mark Enns. "Human Interaction and Cortisol: Can Human Contact Reduce Stress in Shelter Dogs?" *Physiology and Behavior* 87 (2006): 537–41.

Grandin, T. "Case Study: How Horses Helped a Teenager with Autism Make Friends and Learn How to Work." *International Journal of Environmental Research and Public Health* 113 (2019): 2325.

Grandin, T. "My Reflections on Understanding Animal Emotions for Improving the Life of Animals in Zoos." *Journal of Applied Animal Welfare Science* 21 (2018): 12–22.

Grandin, Temple, and Catherine Johnson. *Animals in Translation*. New York: Houghton Mifflin Harcourt, 2006.

Grandin, Temple, and Catherine Johnson. *Animals Make Us Human*. New York: Houghton Mifflin Harcourt, 2006.

Grandin, Temple, and Mark D. Deesing. *Genetics and the Behavior of Domestic Animals*. 2nd ed. San Diego: Elsevier, 2013.

Grandin, Temple. *Temple Grandin's Guide to Working with Farm Animals*. North Adams, M.A.: Storey, 2017.

Grandin, Temple. *Thinking in Pictures*. New York: Vintage, 1996.

Grandin, Temple. www.grandin.com. (Author's website on animal behavior and welfare.)

Phillips, M., T. Grandin, W. Graffam, N. Irlbeck, and R. C. Cambre. "Crate Conditioning of Bongo (Tragelaphus eurycerus) for Veterinary and Husbandry Procedures at Denver Zoological Gardens." *Zoo Biology* 17 (1998): 25–32.

Voisinet, Bridget D., Temple Grandin, et al. "Feedlot Cattle with Calm Temperaments Have Higher Average Daily Gains Than Cattle with Excitable Temperaments." *Journal of Animal Science* 75 (April 1997): 892–96.

CITIZEN SCIENCE SOURCES FOR SCIENCE TEACHERS
(also see Chapter Four: Birds and Chapter Five: The Night Skies)

Garrett, M. P. D., et al. "Capacity and Willingness of Farmers and Citizens to Monitor Crop Pollinators and Pollinator Services." *Global Ecology and Conservation* 20 (2019): e00781.

Lintott, Chris. *The Crowd and the Cosmos*. New York: Oxford University Press, 2020.

Lynch, L. I., et al. "In Their Own Words: The Significance of Participant Percepts in Assessing Entomology Citizen Science Learning Outcomes Using a Mixed Methods Approach." *Insects* 9, no. 1 (2018): 16.

Ryan, S. F., et al. "The Role of Citizen Science in Addressing Grand Challenges in Food and Agriculture Research." *Proceedings of the Royal Society B*, November 21, 2018.

Serret, H., et al. "Data Quality and Participant Engagement in Citizen Science: Two Approaches for Monitoring Pollinators in France and South Korea." *Citizen Science Theory and Practice* 4 (July 18, 2019): 22.

Twitley, N. "With Bugs You Are Never Home Alone." *The New York Times*, October 29, 2019.

INDEX

Note: Page numbers in italics refer to illustrations. Page numbers that are underlined refer to projects.